Doing Right

FROM PROSECUTOR TO REFORMER: A JOURNEY THROUGH CRIME, CORRUPTION, COMPLACENCY, AND CHANGE

JEFF SCHLANGER

This is a work of nonfiction based on the author's recollections, experience, research, and interpretation of events. Certain names and identifying details may have been changed where appropriate for privacy, legal, or narrative purposes.

Any inadvertent errors are unintentional.

Publisher: IntegrAssure Press

Palm Beach, FL

integrassure.com

Library of Congress Control Number: 2026907671

Paperback ISBN: 979-8-9954079-0-4

Hardcover ISBN: 979-8-9954079-1-1

First edition

Dedication

To T, Danielle, Jake, and Drew: You lived through the nights I was away, the days spent in airport lounges, the holidays interrupted by crises, and the moments I missed at home while pursuing the work described in these pages. Your love, patience, and resilience made every chapter of this journey possible. Whatever I accomplished, I accomplished because you all carried the cost.

To Shai, and to my grandchildren yet to come: Your arrival made me want to set down the story of where I have been, what I have seen, and what I tried to stand for. It is my account for you of the life I tried to live, the work I tried to do, and the meaning I hoped it held.

Author's Note

While I have taken care to situate events within their proper historical and factual context, this book is not presented as a strictly chronological account. Certain episodes are organized thematically or narratively rather than sequentially, in service of clarity, coherence, and meaning. The story told here is also drawn from memory spanning more than four decades of professional life, often lived at a relentless pace. To the extent that minor chronological imprecision remains, it is unintentional and reflects the ordinary frailties of human memory rather than any effort to misstate events, diminish their significance, or alter their substance.

Table of Contents

Preface

I have titled this book Doing Right, but I offer that phrase as my aspiration—the standard I strove to meet even when the path was obscured by politics, pressure, or my own fallibility. In more than forty years of navigating the criminal justice system—from the streets of Hell's Kitchen to the command center of the NYPD—I learned that "doing right" is rarely a clear destination. It is a messy, exhausting, and often imperfect discipline.

It is the act of trying to find the ethical path in a system sometimes designed to obscure it, and accepting that, despite your best intentions, you will stumble. This is a story about those stumbles as much as the successes.

It is not simply the story of one life, but of the people and moments that shaped it—moments when institutions faltered, when people surprised me, and when the path forward was anything but clear.

It begins with a family that fled annihilation, and with a boy who grew up learning that the world was more complicated than the stories adults told—especially when it came to the people entrusted to keep others safe. That lesson carried me into courtrooms where I prosecuted the Westies and then John Gotti; into the command centers of the LAPD and NYPD as both cities fought to rebuild trust in the wake of systemic failings; and, eventually, into communities across the country struggling to hold power to account without losing faith in the people behind the badge.

The path was rarely straight. There were moments when what happened seemed to blur, when exhaustion or pressure made even simple decisions feel heavy. But there were also moments of redemption—when courage, empathy, or simple decency turned the tide, if only for a while. Those moments convinced me that "doing right" is less a destination than a discipline—a daily effort made in the face of temptation, fatigue, and fear.

I am deeply grateful to my family, and to the friends, colleagues, and mentors—some named here, many not—whose guidance and example made that journey possible. This book does not recount every case, crisis, or relationship that shaped my life. In time, I hope to create a supplement to certain chapters, chronicling the more personal details and memories that remain quietly sustaining.

For now, I offer this as a record of the places and people that shaped my career—and of the choices that stayed with me long after the courtroom lights dimmed.

Prelude

The Devil We Came to Know

When Jimmy McElroy took the stand on that February morning in 1990, I'd already spent months with him in the makeshift facility we'd built at the State University of New York Maritime College, beneath the Throgs Neck Bridge. It had become his sanctuary—and our own improvised version of a witness protection program. We'd taken him out of federal custody to answer for pending state charges, and when he agreed to cooperate, we built the facility to keep him safe, close, and talking.

His testimony had the potential to unravel years of violence and expose alliances that even seasoned investigators had only suspected.

Night after night, we went through the case, word by word, until the mythology of loyalty thinned and he crossed over—from soldier to witness. It was a strange arrangement: part interrogation, part confession. The days blurred into nights as we sat across from each other at a folding table, the water's echo in the distance, with two of my detectives always watching. Each session felt like a race against time—a fight to keep him committed, lucid, and protected long enough to tell the jury what he knew.

He was angry—at the federal prosecutors who had convicted him, at the judge who had sentenced him to sixty years, and at his former cronies who had turned on him to save themselves. He knew that cooperation wasn't merely a legal risk but a mortal one, and every answer he gave carried a price. His cooperation with us was as much about settling that score as it was about building a case. Yet beneath the bitterness was the exhaustion of a man who had done monstrous things—who had cut up more bodies than he could remember and carried those memories like the smell of bleach on his skin. McElroy was a killer who had come to see that the code he'd lived by no longer protected him, and that telling what he knew might be the only leverage he had left.

When he finally walked into the courtroom, it felt as if we were leading a man out of the shadows and into the sun. The place was packed—reporters, sketch artists, television cameras, and the hum of whispers following every movement at the defense table. John Gotti sat immaculate, cufflinks glinting under the fluorescent lights, exuding the calm of a man who believed the room already belonged to him.

McElroy took his seat in the witness box, no longer the enforcer from Hell's Kitchen, but a man stripped of everything except the story he was about to tell. For months, we had prepared him for this moment, but even then, watching him raise his hand to take the oath, I wondered which would prove stronger—his anger or his fear.

He started slowly, his voice even but tight, like a man learning a new language after years of silence. He told the story we had rehearsed so many times: the meeting after Frank DeCicco's wake; the message passed through Jimmy Coonan that "the carpenter had to be taught a lesson"; the plan drawn up in a neighborhood bar; and the shots that left John O'Connor bleeding on the floor of 1650 Broadway. There was no flourish, no attempt to justify—just a dry chronology of violence, delivered by the man who had carried it out.

Every word seemed to cost him something—not because of guilt, but because violence had become his native tongue, and he was now struggling to speak another. Beside me sat Mike Cherkasky—my boss, my friend, and now the lead prosecutor on the case I had started and that we, together with our team, were about to carry to its natural conclusion. I had set the wheels in motion years earlier with the prosecution of the Westies' second-in-command, Mickey Featherstone, and that road had led us here, to a courtroom where facts had to fight for air.

Cross-examination turned the courtroom into a carnival of aggression. Bruce Cutler came at McElroy with the full force of his personality—the swagger, the volume, the contempt that had become part of the Gotti legend. He called McElroy a liar, a coward, a murderer trading testimony for salvation. He pounded the table, jabbed a finger and shouted over objections. The judge tried to rein him in, but Cutler knew exactly what he was doing: he wasn't questioning the facts; he was performing for the jury's doubts.

McElroy didn't answer in kind. He sat there, expressionless, letting the insults land, then quietly repeated that he had done what he was told—and that now he was telling the jury exactly what that had been. For a man who had once taken orders to butcher bodies, his restraint was chilling: violence replaced by a fatal calm. He wasn't eloquent, but he was real—and in that moment, real felt like the rarest thing in the room.

Weeks before the trial began, Mike and I had sat across from the FBI agents who'd been pursuing Gotti for years, as they assured us that if they heard anything on their wire at the Ravenite Social Club—anything at all about interference with the jury—they would alert us immediately. We believed them. The bugs were theirs; the intelligence was theirs; the promise seemed straightforward.

The jury deliberated for days, shut away from the world while the rest of the city waited. Each morning, as we walked through the security gauntlet into the courthouse, the press lined the steps and shouted the same questions: How's it looking? Any word? We gave them nothing—mostly because there was nothing to give. Then, late on a Friday afternoon, the word came. The jury had reached a verdict.

We stood as the clerk read it—not guilty on all counts. The pit in my stomach, which came just before the reading of any verdict, turned to nausea. Gotti straightened his tie, smiled, and turned toward the gallery like a man accepting an award. By the time we stepped outside, the celebration had already begun: fireworks over Ozone Park, champagne at the Ravenite. For him, it was vindication. For us, it was silence.

Throughout the trial we had stayed alert, trusting that if anyone tried to reach a juror, we'd know. We didn't. Only well after the verdict did we learn what had really happened: that a juror had been tampered with, that an officer from the NYPD's Intelligence Division had helped make it happen, and that the FBI had known as our trial—and the plot to influence that juror—unfolded. What had felt like a loss in court revealed itself, over time, to be something worse: a betrayal from inside the very institutions we were relying on to keep the process clean.

In the weeks that followed, the courthouse emptied, the headlines faded, and the city returned to its uneasy rhythm. But something had shifted for me. I realized that the drama we had just lived wasn't just about a verdict. It was a collision of individual journeys, and the courtroom had been the cauldron of those colliding lives, each person pulled there by their own unbroken thread of circumstance. From the bench to the defense table, every person in that room was the product of a thousand variables—choices made, corners turned, and loyalties tested. Whether driven by ambition, duty, violence, or the law, we were all tethered to the paths that brought us together in that courtroom.

Every one of us has the journey that we have traveled: a single, unbroken thread that starts in some childhood room and ends wherever the variables finally drop us. Shift the neighborhood, the decade, the father who walked out, or the cop who looked the other way, and the same thread might have carried any of us to the witness stand, the prosecution table, or the defendant's dock. Some become monsters. Some spend their careers chasing it.

Institutions, too, have threads. Lurking beneath us was the invisible thread of institutional failure—the corrupt cop and the silent agents—proving that the guardians themselves could be turned against justice.

Understanding how those threads get twisted—and whose hands can prevent that twisting or untangle them once the damage is done—is what, in one form or another, I have tried to grasp ever since.

This book follows my thread: the path of a boy raised on the quiet, tree-lined streets of Valley Stream, who had come to that courtroom believing that if you worked hard enough and dug deep enough, the truth would matter. It explores the intersection of my journey and the threads of people—and institutions—I met along the way.

To follow that thread to that courtroom, and into everything that came after, we have to go back. Back to the beginning.

Chapter 1
Where It Began

Doing right isn't always complicated—until the moment it truly counts. Power, fear, and ambition can warp judgment in ways you don't see coming. I learned that long before I sat across from John Gotti. To understand how a boy from Valley Stream ended up there, we have to go back to the quiet streets where lessons weren't taught so much as absorbed.

I grew up in a family shaped by escape, reinvention, and the understanding that the law could protect or destroy depending on whose hands controlled it. At home, values weren't speeches; they were habits—small acts of steadiness and decency that told you what mattered without ever naming it.

Those lessons began before I was born, on the dark streets of Vienna during the night the world would come to know as Kristallnacht—the Night of Broken Glass. My mother, Litza Koppelmann—Lizzi, before America offered her a new beginning—was fourteen when the mobs came. The windows of Jewish homes and businesses shattered under boots and rifle butts, shards glittering across a city sliding into violence. Her father, Jacob—for whom I was named using the first letter of his name—knew they had to leave. Soon after, they fled Vienna with her mother, Suzie, and her sister, Thea. Their passage to America was narrow, made possible only because Suzie's brother had immigrated years earlier and could sponsor them.

Millions of others were not so fortunate. Many members of our extended family perished in the Holocaust, their faces and names remembered only in stories and in the empty spaces where they should have been.

I was raised in the shadow of that escape. As a child, I didn't understand its weight, but my mother carried it quietly. The Holocaust wasn't a single revelation; it lived in the background of family conversations. Each mention of those we lost made clear that harm, when ignored, has a way of spreading. It also created a specific kind of quiet in our house. My parents didn't talk about "justice" in the abstract; they focused on survival and stability. I learned early that when the rules break down, people like us are the first to suffer. That anxiety was never spoken aloud, but it was the hum in the air I grew up breathing.

My mother's life in America was built on talent and on people who recognized it. She arrived without a word of English and finished high school in two years. A Protestant teacher at Paterson High School, Mrs. Grebe, saw her potential and secured aid for her to attend Grinnell College, where she graduated Phi Beta Kappa.

In the 1950s, my mother's career in import-export set her apart. While most women in our neighborhood stayed home, she spent her days in a Manhattan office alive with the clatter of typewriters and the shuffle of global trade. She rose through the ranks, eventually earning an equity stake in her company—a rare achievement for a woman of her generation.

Sometimes she brought me with her. I'd watch her navigate deals with a quiet confidence that seemed to steady the room. Those days sparked a curiosity about how systems worked—and about the people who kept them running.

My father, Sam, brought a different kind of steadiness to our home. Born in Chicago during the Depression, he was shaped by scarcity and determination. He attended the Merchant Marine Academy at Kings Point, earned a commission as a Navy lieutenant junior grade, ferried supplies across the Atlantic during the war, and then entered Cooper Union, the fiercely competitive engineering school that offered free tuition to those who earned it.

He spent his career in aerospace, designing components for the Space Shuttle and military equipment—a field that demanded precision and imagination. Even in his late seventies, he commuted an hour each way, believing deeply that work wasn't a burden, but a privilege.

The Depression taught him to value every penny and every hour. "Nothing comes free," he'd say, tinkering with his latest project in the basement, his tools arranged with military order. He met my mother during his service, introduced by a friend who happened to be dating her at the time. Something sparked. They married in 1944, blending her Viennese resilience with his Midwestern grit, and built a life grounded in perseverance—the beginning of how I came to understand the world.

My sister, Deborah—Debby—was three years younger. She now lives on the West Coast with her wife having raised their two adopted daughters from Guatemala. Her determination to live openly, despite the prejudices of her time, echoed our parents' defiance of history and reinforced something simple: people deserved space to be who they were.

We settled in Valley Stream, Long Island—a suburb on the Queens border carved from farmland in the postwar boom. Green Acres, our neighborhood, was tidy and overwhelmingly Jewish, with its own school and a sense of insulation from the turmoil of the wider world.

To manage the home while my mother worked, we had a housekeeper, Hannah Smith—a warm, steady woman from Bed-Stuy by way of North Carolina. She was more than help; she was family. On some Sundays, she took me—a little Jewish boy—to her Black Baptist church, where the choir's gospel hymns lifted the rafters. I learned "Amazing Grace" there, years before I'd hear it played at police funerals.

When I was seven, I overheard Hannah telling my mother, tears in her voice, "My grandson Eddie's been shot." Eddie, a teenager, had been caught in an altercation in Bed-Stuy and barely survived. The tremor in her hands as she dusted the shelves stayed with me. It was my first glimpse of the kind of violence I would later confront in Manhattan courtrooms—and of the endurance people carried without ever announcing it.

November 22, 1963: I was ten, doodling in class when the

loudspeaker cracked. President Kennedy was dead. At home, the television flickered with Oswald's murder, live. History split open on the screen. Only a few years later, Martin Luther King Jr. and Robert Kennedy would be assassinated. The riots following King's death sent cities into flames. My mother's face tightened at the news, as though history's shadows were catching up.

Even before that, the wider world felt unsettled. We ducked under desks for civil defense drills, pretending thin wood could shield us from nuclear fire. We memorized color-coded evacuation routes, as if preparation alone could hold back catastrophe.

My early heroes were figures of imagination and fairness—Superman, Batman, Green Lantern, and The Flash. But looking back, it wasn't the flying or other super-powers that drew me in; it was the clarity. In the comic books, unlike the confusing world of the 1960s, right and wrong were distinct boundaries. I was drawn to the idea of a protector—someone who stepped in not to cause chaos, but to restore order when the system failed.

That notion found a real-world echo in the Boy Scout Oath. "On my honor, I will do my best..." became a pledge that stuck with me, well past my stint with Troop 167, which was shortened by Star Trek, with its vision of diplomacy over force, that aired Monday nights opposite scout meetings. The Starship Enterprise, exploring new worlds and going where no man had gone before, won out over the troop.

I absorbed my parents' lessons about work and self-reliance. At eleven, I started a paper route, pedaling before dawn to deliver the morning news. At fourteen, with working papers in hand, I took jobs at the Green Acres Shopping Center—stocking shelves, selling shoes, and eventually working security at Alexander's. The summer I turned fifteen, my mother found me a job at a freight forwarder in Battery Park—my first taste of Manhattan and independence. I would drive with my father, who was working in New Jersey at the time, and get dropped off at the Jerome Avenue Station and take the 4 train to Battery Park.

Once I could drive, I worked at The Woodrow, a local deli—bussing tables, then delivering platters of pastrami, tongue, and corned beef to families celebrating or mourning. Work became more than just hours; it became an identity.

But work didn't shield me from the divisions beyond Green Acres. To reach Valley Stream South Junior/Senior High School, where sixth graders from four grammar schools in Valley Stream combined, you crossed Hook Creek Bridge—a literal and symbolic boundary between our Jewish enclave of Green Acres and its Forest Road School and the predominantly Christian neighborhoods beyond. Swastikas sometimes appeared on the bridge. High-school fraternities excluded Jewish students. After one school dance, a fraternity boy punched me and muttered, "Jew."

Small moments, but they stayed with me. They showed how quickly things could turn—and how fragile dignity could be.

The 1960s fractured the country. The Civil Rights Movement surged, Vietnam split households, and the nightly news toggled between marches and body counts. Watching marchers beaten and jailed yet unbroken, I began to understand something simple: the world didn't set itself right without people insisting on it.

In 1969, division reached our own high school. Students fought over whether to lower the flag to half-staff in protest of Vietnam. I watched from the edge, unsure then where I would stand when it truly mattered.

That same year, at sixteen, I hitchhiked to Woodstock. I found rain, mud, and enough music to make the chaos feel briefly hopeful. Under gray skies, Hendrix's guitar screamed a fractured anthem for a country at war with itself. I returned home soaked but steadier, believing that some fights mattered more than others.

Later, at an anti-war rally, someone hit me with an egg. The yolk slid down my jacket as the crowd's chants swallowed my first instinct to swing back. A stranger's voice—"Stay peaceful"—caught me. I saw how easily anger could make you forget why you'd shown up in the first place. That chaotic energy—the screaming, the anger, the fracturing of certainty—was frightening to me. While some of my peers were drawn to the revolution, I found myself looking for the guardrails. I didn't want to burn the system down; I wanted to understand the mechanics of how it could be fixed so that it didn't have to burn. I didn't know it then, but I was already looking for the structure that the law provides.

Wrestling for the Valley Stream South Falcons—freshman, junior varsity, varsity—taught me endurance: offense and defense at once, the will to resist while advancing. I wasn't by any stretch gifted, but I was relentless. Wrestling demanded persistence and humility—traits that would matter more in courtrooms than strength ever could. Wrestling is the most honest sport there is because there is no one else to blame. If you lose, you can't blame the goalie or the quarterback; you were simply outmaneuvered. That solitary accountability appealed to me. It was the perfect training for a life in the law, where, at the end of the day, it is just you, the facts, and the judge. You can't hide in a scrum.

My parents never came to my matches. It wasn't neglect; that just wasn't how things worked then. My father was working, and my mother was always in motion. I understood—but still wished they'd been there, just once.

The lessons from the mat followed me elsewhere: in standing up to bullies, walking a picket line, arguing in class. There was always the same tension—the urge to push and the need to hold steady.

At the beginning, there was only this: a boy standing at the edge of a new world, carrying the echoes of an old one. He didn't know he would spend his life confronting institutions as often as individuals. He didn't yet understand how easily systems could falter, or how often the hardest battles weren't fought in courtrooms at all. He only knew that, coming from people who survived the unimaginable, you learned to show up—imperfectly, quietly—and try to make things better where you could.

That boy would become a prosecutor, then a reformer, and eventually something harder to define.

I didn't yet know that the distance between Valley Stream and the life of a prosecutor was shorter than I thought—or that the values of that quiet suburb would be the armor I needed to survive the years ahead.

Chapter 2
Independence

The car was a battered 1964 Chevy Impala, a hand-me-down from my parents. It was a little worn around the edges, but to me it might as well have been a golden chariot. It carried me out of the familiar rhythms of suburban life and into the wider world beyond.

In the summer of 1971, just after my eighteenth birthday, I packed a duffel bag, said a quick goodbye, and headed north to the Catskills, driving to the songs of Carole King and James Taylor on the Chevy's AM-radio. My destination was Spring Lake Spa in Parksville, a modest hotel tucked into the wooded hills of Sullivan County, one of the countless resorts that had defined New York's Borscht Belt.

It was not glamorous, but it felt like freedom.

My friend Gary and his parents had worked there before. He returned as a waiter, a job of brutal early mornings and long, relentless shifts. I was luckier: Max, the owner, hired me as the hotel's chauffeur. He seemed to like me, said the hotel needed a driver, but warned that the pay would not match a waiter's. Max had once wrestled at Cornell. He carried himself with the quiet confidence the sport teaches and, together with his wife, Kay, ran the hotel with a calm that made his point clear without raising his voice. I remember the sage advice he provided about the job requirements and Parksville roads: "Just keep it between the ditches and the guests happy—that's all you need to know."

My duties were simple but liberating. I ferried guests to the nearby towns of Parksville and Liberty, sometimes down to Monticello for the race track, and occasionally, for a VIP, all the way back to the city. I loved the driving itself, the sense of motion and agency, the way the sun cut through the trees as the road opened in front of me.

The Catskills still carried traces of an earlier glamour. For decades, Jewish-run hotels had given working- and middle-class families a refuge from city life and discrimination: hearty food, nightly entertainment, a common language spoken in punchlines and pastrami. Comedians sharpened their acts there. Even though the glory days were behind it, the Catskills still featured comedians honing their skills with Yiddish-infused humor. Jerry Lewis, Buddy Hackett, and Henny Youngman continued to appear.

By 1971 the luster had begun to dim. Even so, for a teenager from Valley Stream it was another world. Days at Spring Lake Spa settled into a rhythm of easy conversations, small responsibilities, and the beginnings of real autonomy.

Gary and I shared a small room in the staff quarters, a world unto itself. The workers were a mix of college students, locals, and seasoned staff who returned year after year.

Life in the staff quarters was lively and unpredictable. Friendships formed quickly, often over late-night card games or quiet conversations on the back steps. There were romances as well, some fleeting, others lasting beyond the summer.

The work could be exhausting, especially on weekends when the hotel was packed. I drove guests from morning until late at night, steering the winding mountain roads and dodging the occasional deer.

There was a rhythm to it and a satisfaction in knowing I was trusted to get people where they needed to go. Looking back, that summer taught me more than how to drive a hotel car. I learned responsibility, how to read people, and how to find my place in an unfamiliar setting. It was a small chapter, but it gave me my first real taste of independence.

By late summer, it was time to move on. The car that had carried me north now carried Gary and me west toward a new chapter: college.

We pointed the Impala toward SUNY Binghamton, then still widely known as Harpur College and regarded as the crown jewel of New York State's public university system. I had been accepted to Northwestern, Tufts, and Clark as well, all excellent private schools, but tuition loomed large. Knowing I wanted law school later, I chose a top-tier public university for my undergraduate years and saved the splurge for graduate school. I have never regretted that decision.

Gary and I had asked to live in the same dorm but specifically requested not to be roommates, a small assertion of independence. Housing missed the nuance. We arrived to find ourselves assigned to the same small room, tripled up with a third roommate who would find another room after a few months. Rooming with Gary, however, was a twist that would define our first year.

The campus sat among hills and rivers in upstate New York, green and expansive, serious in its design. As I hung my first poster of Bob Dylan on the cinder block walls and set up my turntable and speakers, it felt far from everything I had known, certainly a major part of the appeal.

It was 1971, and the spirit of change still pulsed through American life. The Vietnam War dragged on. The Pentagon Papers had been leaked, laying bare years of government deception. College campuses simmered with activism. Civil-rights battles continued in the courts and the streets. The counterculture was fading, but its imprint remained.

Within days, tragedy struck in New York State: the Attica prison uprising. On September 9, 1971, inmates demanding better living conditions and basic human rights seized control of the prison. Four days later, a chaotic retaking by state police left 43 prisoners and staff dead. The brutality ignited protests across the country, including on our campus.

At Binghamton, students gathered in anger and sorrow, staging protests and teach-ins. I stood in the crowds and listened. I absorbed the language of injustice and state power, and the bitter taste of betrayal when the government fails its people. I did not know it then, but those lessons would echo across my life and foreshadow roles in which I would oversee and scrutinize law enforcement itself.

Wrestling remained a thread. I loved the sport and knew its reality: sweat, bruises, and discipline. I wanted to keep going.

Wrestling was never the glamorized world of television heroes like Cowboy Bill Watts, Bruno Sammartino, or Argentina Apollo. College wrestling was raw, exhausting, and humbling. My path to the team ran through Coach Steve Erber, who had visited Long Island and South High School on a recruiting trip. As I have said, I was far from the most gifted athlete, but he must have seen something he respected: perhaps perseverance.

That spirit was tested quickly. My weight class—the one I normally wrestled—was already held by a New York State high-school champion. The team needed a heavyweight. To meet the need, I moved up not one or two classes but four. The opponents were larger and stronger, built for the upper brackets. I agreed anyway. The team needed someone willing to try.

The campus newspaper wrote a line about me that made the bruises feel worth it: "He may not be the best wrestler on the team, but he is certainly the bravest."

Bravery, I learned, does not shield you from physics. The mismatches were punishing and the damage cumulative. During my sophomore year I injured my back in a match. I did not grasp at first how serious it was. I was in pain, could not stand for long, and walking grew difficult. I could not wrestle, but I convinced myself I could keep doing other things.

One of those things was riding the Vespa I had bought from my teammate Rick Pari, a kind soul who, tragically, would take his own life two years later. The suspension was terrible and the bouncing certainly did not help. I also joined old high-school friends for a winter-break trip to Miami Beach. We crammed into a budget motel on Collins Avenue, expecting nothing worse than sunburn and bad food. One morning I woke up unable to move my legs. No sensation. No strength. Only the cold stillness of fear. The ceiling tiles were blurred; I counted them to stay calm. An ambulance was called, and I waved goodbye to my friends as they took me away.

At Parkway General Hospital, the doctors were clear: I needed spinal surgery soon, and there was a chance I might not walk again. These were the days before MRIs. The diagnostic test was a myelogram: dye injected into the spinal column, the table tilted so the dye could trace its path under X-ray. It was agonizing.

My mother flew down from New York immediately. My father, for reasons I still do not fully understand, did not. The surgery succeeded, but recovery was grueling. I returned to New York medicated, diminished, and exhausted. Wrestling—as a competitive pursuit—was over. I took a leave of absence for the second semester of my sophomore year, then returned and graduated with the rest of my class and with honors in May 1975. I still have the occasional nightmare about not finishing, although I know I did.

In the first days after surgery, it felt in many ways like the end of who I thought I was, but clearly it was not. Life went on and in many ways was enriched.

At the beginning of sophomore year, I had moved off campus with three teammates—Wally, Louie, and Billy. We pooled our meager resources and bought a 12-foot-wide mobile home for $3,000 in a trailer park a mile from campus in Vestal. It had three bedrooms, rationally speaking clearly not enough for four young men. Yet, Wally and Billy split a king-size waterbed to make it work.

Before long the mobile home became more than a place to sleep. It was a world of our own: four wrestlers, two dogs (an Irish Setter and a German Shepherd), a shifting cast of girlfriends, music, arguments, and laughter. By any reasonable adult measure, it was chaos. It was also where I recovered from surgery.

To make ends meet, I took a job driving the college's off-campus bus, making rounds through Vestal, Johnson City, and downtown Binghamton. The bus was a relic from the 1950s that required double-clutching to shift properly. Drawing on my Catskills chauffeuring experience, I navigated narrow, icy streets in that green beast of a bus, which was an education in responsibility and patience. Later, I picked up routes with the Schaeffer Bus Company, driving commercial runs for high-school teams and cheerleaders. I was eighteen. Today, that would be hard to imagine.

Service took another form as well. In 1972, only weeks into the semester, I joined an EMT training course which I stumbled upon in my dorm, Broome Hall. It was part of the groundwork for what became one of the first student-run emergency medical services in the country: Harpur's Ferry Ambulance Corps. I was among its founding members.

We trained rigorously to handle real emergencies: stabilizing fractures, clearing airways, calming panicked patients, and making split-second decisions. We staffed the ambulance day and night, responding on campus and in the surrounding community. It was not glamorous work. It was real—broken bones, overdoses, asthma attacks, heart palpitations, alcohol poisonings. The stakes were immediate; the lessons endured.

Through Harpur's Ferry I found paid work with a local private company, Tri-Cities Ambulance. The company was owned by the area funeral home and served as a primary responder for the Broome County Sheriff. Tri-Cities had sold Harpur's Ferry its first ambulance, a converted hearse for $125. At Tri-Cities, we responded to calls ranging from routine transports to full trauma responses, some of which remain with me to this day.

One call ended any fascination I had with motorcycles. A man crashed at high speed; the gas tank exploded, engulfing his leg in flames.

When we reached Binghamton General Hospital the smell of gasoline still hung in the air. As the doctors removed his boot, flesh came away with it. A month later we transported him again, this time to a rehabilitation facility where, as a new amputee, he began the long process of learning to walk again.

For a time, I considered applying to become a campus police officer, drawn by the same instinct to serve and to stand for something larger than myself. In the end, for reasons I no longer recall, I never filed the application.

What being an EMT taught me most was presence. You show up when someone is at their worst and do your best to help. No accolades. No speeches. You answer the call because someone has to.

Those years—marked by injuries, friendships, challenges, and the quiet work of showing up when needed—gave me an education no classroom could offer. The boy who once crossed the Hook Creek bridge to get to high school was now navigating something wider: new places, new responsibilities, and the early sense that the world was larger and more complicated than he'd imagined. I didn't see it then, but the shape of the life ahead was beginning to take form.

Chapter 3
The Vocation

By the end of college, one question had come into focus: What kind of life was I going to build?

I had tasted independence. I had shouldered real responsibility—from wrestling mats to ambulance calls, from double-clutching off-campus buses to standing in the middle of protests. I had seen a nation divided by war, injustice, and doubt.

The next step couldn't simply be about chasing money or status. I believed it had to be about meaning—about protecting the vulnerable and trying to foster fairness in what to me was a chaotic world. The law offered that path.

But the law in the 1970s was not seen with the reverence it once commanded. The country was still reeling from Watergate and revelations that the highest offices in the land had betrayed the public trust. Vietnam had shattered the idea of unquestioning loyalty to the government. Movements for civil rights and women's rights had exposed how often the law served to protect privilege rather than justice. Skepticism about authority was everywhere—and rightly so.

Yet for me, that made the pursuit of law more important, not less. I didn't believe in abandoning the system. I believed in making it better—by working within it, demanding more from it, and never forgetting who it was supposed to serve. I considered a career in policing. But it was lawyers, I realized, who ultimately shaped society.

Some of that realization was formed years earlier, sitting beside my mother in our living room as we adjusted the TV antenna and watched Perry Mason, the television series centered on the courtroom brilliance of its titular defense attorney. It wasn't Mason, though, who held my attention, but rather, Hamilton

Burger—the beleaguered District Attorney who rose each episode to make the case for accountability. Even as a boy, I sensed there was something noble in that role: standing up, day after day, not for the accused, but for the people. I somehow recognized that someone must make the case for truth and justice. I later wrote about those evenings—about rooting for the prosecutor—in my law school application essay.

Despite completing my undergraduate studies in seven semesters—truncated by injury and recovery—my GPA was high and I scored very well on the LSATs, enough to make me a candidate for the top-tier law schools. I applied broadly: accepted to Northwestern and NYU; rejected from Yale and Harvard. After weighing my options, I chose NYU Law School. It felt like the right fit—renowned for its intellectual rigor, steeped in public service tradition, and firmly grounded in the energy of New York City, which I already considered home. It was a place where I believed I could grow not only as a student of the law, but as someone committed to using that law in the service of something greater than myself.

Situated in the heart of Greenwich Village, it thrived at the intersection of activism and academia—a place where the nation's hardest questions were tested daily. I wasn't looking for prestige. I was looking for purpose. Without fully realizing it, I had already started down a path that would define the rest of my life.

Though many of my classmates lived in the NYU dorms surrounding Washington Square Park, I opted for something different. I found a small rental apartment on West 24th Street between Eighth and Ninth Avenues, just across from the London Terrace apartments. It was a modest one-bedroom, and I planned to share it by subletting the living room. I posted a note on an NYU board, and a woman attending Rutgers Law School answered the ad. She moved in, kept to herself, and we coexisted as compatible, if distant, roommates. What remains clearest in my memory is the block itself. This was the pre–pooper-scooper era in New York, and the sidewalks of West 24th Street were a minefield—dodging dog feces became a daily exercise in agility and awareness.

That block felt like a small emblem of the city's frayed edges—messy, unvarnished, and honest—reminding me daily that much of my work would be about confronting disorder head-on.

My first year at NYU was a baptism by fire. The Socratic method, the endless casebook reading, and the intensity of the classroom exchanges defined the experience. The curriculum was traditional: Torts, Contracts, Civil Procedure, Criminal Law, and Criminal Procedure. Although our incoming class was divided into three sections, I have lasting relationships with many from all three sections, including Mark Speed, who would eventually become my law partner, and Moshe Sukenik, who, despite taking an extra year to finish law school, remains one of my dearest friends.

After the first year, I moved out of 24th Street and into a newly opened apartment complex on the far west side of the Village. It was a sprawling four-bedroom duplex walk-up. The rent was $513.64—a figure I still remember, not only because it was so exact, but also because, even then, it was a steal. I moved in with Moshe, Vinny, and another section mate, Dennis. It was a quintessential New York setup: a group of aspiring lawyers living modestly but ambitiously in a city that demanded both resilience and imagination. The bohemian West Village became our stomping grounds, and free time was spent in the myriad bars and musical venues.

NYU was intense, challenging, and defiantly left of center.

The Criminal Law Clinic, where I spent much of my second and third years, emphasized defense work almost exclusively, encouraging students to see themselves as protectors against the excesses of state power.

It was the most valuable part of law school—not because it changed my goals, but because it sharpened my understanding of how fragile justice could be. Learning how defense attorneys viewed the system—how they spotted weakness and unfairness—made me a better, more thoughtful advocate for the rule of law. I learned about the art of cross-examination, which would serve me particularly well in my prosecutorial career, as generally, prosecutors are poor cross-examiners.

As my second-year summer was approaching, I applied for NYU's stipend program aimed at promoting public service work. My choice of work was at the Manhattan District Attorney's Office, but the school refused to grant the stipend. Prosecution, I was told, was not public service. I remember staring in disbelief. That moment crystallized something in me: that justice—and what constituted service to the public—was in the eye of the beholder.

To this day, my relationship with NYU is shaped by that early judgment.

Despite not getting the stipend, I took the unpaid internship at the Manhattan District Attorney's Office.

The Manhattan District Attorney's Office was—and remains—one of the most storied prosecutorial offices in the world. Founded in 1801, it had, over nearly two centuries, established a reputation for fearless independence and relentless pursuit of justice.

By the time I arrived, Robert Morgenthau had been DA for just a few years, but he had already stamped the Office with his own brand of integrity, toughness, and public service. A former U.S. Attorney for the Southern District of New York, Morgenthau had built his career prosecuting organized crime, public corruption, and white-collar offenses long before such cases captured headlines.

Morgenthau, known simply as "The Boss," was demanding but fair—a leader who expected his assistants to be ethical and fearless, and who gave them room to grow, sometimes by fire. The Office was guided by one overriding principle: Do the right thing.

The Office was housed, at what was then 155 Leonard Street, the side wing of the post-depression Manhattan Criminal Court, a no-nonsense building on the edge of Chinatown. It would later be renamed One Hogan Place in honor of the legendary District Attorney Frank Hogan, who had led the Office for more than three decades before the then-current DA, Robert Morgenthau.

The summer of 1977 turned out to be one of the most fateful summers in New York City history. In July, the Great Northeast Blackout plunged the city into darkness. For twenty-five hours, chaos reigned: looting, arson, violence. Entire neighborhoods burned, exposing just how thin the veneer of civil order could be.

At the same time, the city was gripped by fear of the Son of Sam, David Berkowitz, a serial killer who prowled the streets with a 44-caliber revolver, murdering young couples seemingly at random. The terror only deepened when he left cryptic notes taunting the police and the media. The Son of Sam investigation was led by Joe Borelli, who would eventually become Chief of Detectives at the NYPD and, after his retirement, work for me.

During those summer months, I explored Chinatown, drifting through dim sum parlors and narrow lanes that smelled of ginger and incense. Sometimes a date met me; we'd eat in Chinatown, then watch arraignments—a ritual that seemed natural then.

After the blackout, I was assigned to the Early Case Assessment Bureau (ECAB), where I spent hours writing up looting affidavits by hand. I met Assistant District Attorneys who would become lifelong friends and colleagues. In the middle of the city's fear and upheaval, I found a sense of belonging I hadn't fully anticipated.

Inside the DA's Office, the city's chaos narrowed to paper and pen: flickering lights, the scrape of chairs, and the slow ache of a hand cramped from drafting affidavit after affidavit. It was my first clear glimpse of how vital—and how unglamorous—justice work could be.

I met Robert Morgenthau himself more than once—the District Attorney who, with his craggy voice and implacable demeanor, embodied both toughness and fairness. Morgenthau carried his own family's legacy: he was the son of Henry Morgenthau Jr., FDR's Secretary of the Treasury and an early advocate for European Jews and Armenians facing persecution. His friendship with the

Kennedys, forged in shared public service, lent him a quiet gravitas that resonated beyond the courthouse.

I can still hear the gravel in his voice, see the stack of well-worn files on his desk, and feel the pause before he spoke—a silence that managed to be both scrutiny and welcome.

I quickly learned that the men and women around me worked not for glory, but to keep the city stitched together when it seemed ready to tear itself apart. That summer solidified my resolve. This was where I belonged—not in classrooms debating theory, but in courtrooms fighting for real justice.

I applied to return to 155 Leonard Street—this time not as an intern, but as an Assistant District Attorney, standing up in the courtroom "For the People." When my offer letter arrived, the starting salary was $12,500 a year. Before I walked through the door, the Office raised it to $13,000, which felt like a windfall at the time. Even so, it was hardly enough to live on in Manhattan. Most of us shared apartments, skipped meals, and learned to stretch a dollar as far as it would go. No one was there for the money. The work carried its own pull, and we accepted the financial reality as part of the bargain.

I was assigned to Trial Bureau 44, a unit that handled everything from prostitution and gambling to homicides, with cases assigned based on an assistant's experience and growth.

The Office was shifting toward a vertical prosecution model, soon redesignating Bureau 44 as Trial Bureau 60, one of six trial bureaus that operated identically, alongside specialized bureaus of Appeals, Frauds, and Rackets. The vertical model meant prosecutors handled a case—whether petty larceny or homicide—from arrest through conviction, owning it from start to finish, living with its complexities and its consequences.

It was a crucible—a place where the only way to learn was to do.

I felt the weight of responsibility—not only for the cases in my care, but for the faith that the system could still work when handled with precision and integrity. That belief became my compass.

In those early years, I found a small community that would become the foundation of my professional life. Chris Chang, my first officemate, became one of my closest friends. Also in that bureau were two other men who would remain dear to me: Jimmy Friel, whose humor and decency lit every room, and Bob Silbering, who became my "rabbi" in the Office and later in life. Jimmy's death from spinal meningitis at forty-nine left a hole that never fully closed. And Bob and I, all these years later, still gather in Florida with our wives to play canasta and remember those days.

The first year was shaped by the Misdemeanor Trial Program—a baptism by fire. Forty or so new hires competed to see how many misdemeanor cases they could try to a verdict. It wasn't formalized with trophies or awards, but everyone knew who the leaders were. I found myself among them, alongside Mike Cherkasky, who had entered the DA's Office the same day I did, and Chris Chang.

Mike and I quickly became friendly adversaries, a relationship that would evolve into a lifelong friendship and partnership. We were drawn to the competition by a shared love of trial work and a stubborn refusal to back down from tough cases.

Our days were spent in courtrooms—handling petty thefts, assaults, drunken brawls—each one a small but meaningful battle in the larger war for public trust.

It was gritty and real—the scent of burnt coffee and old paper, officers trading stories in scuffed hallways, and the fates of strangers turning on a handful of words.

My days were long, my nights often longer, a rhythm I embraced because each file, each witness, and each cross-examination was another step toward mastering the craft.

My nights often ended at Forlini's, tucked just off Baxter

Street at the edge of Chinatown. Mike, a teetotaler who was more reserved by temperament, always headed home to his wife, Betsy and their newborn child. But Forlini's became my gathering place.

It wasn't just a bar. It was an extension of the criminal justice system itself—messy, human, complicated, and strangely enduring. On any evening, the bar and booths might hold prosecutors, defense attorneys, detectives, and a few familiar faces from nearby Little Italy whose interests didn't exactly align with law enforcement. Deals were struck. Stories were swapped. And occasionally, a sideways glance reminded you that not everyone there was on the same side of the law.

What I couldn't fully appreciate at the time was how many of my peers would go on to shape the future. In the few years surrounding my entry into the Office, a roster of names appeared on the rookie Assistant DA lists:

- Eliot Spitzer, who would become Attorney General and Governor of New York.

-Sonia Sotomayor, who would rise to the United States Supreme Court.

-Cyrus Vance Jr., who would eventually succeed Morgenthau as DA and become one of my best friends.

-Andrew Cuomo, who would serve as Attorney General and Governor.

-John F. Kennedy Jr., who would leave his own complicated mark before his tragic death.

-Robert F. Kennedy Jr., who would become Secretary of Health and Human Services in the Trump administration.

At the time, we were simply young lawyers trying to prove ourselves. But looking back, it feels as if history itself passed through those halls. We brushed shoulders and shared trial stories over coffee in the cafeteria, affectionately known as "The Roach

Coach."

The Manhattan DA's Office wasn't just a job. It was a forge. Those early years—bruising, exhilarating, demanding—would shape not just my career, but my character.

The boy from Valley Stream—son of a refugee who fled extinction at the hands of the Nazis—had arrived at one of the nation's most influential prosecutorial offices determined to do more than win: to do right, especially when it mattered most.

Chapter 4
The Rookie

The next lessons would not come from professors or casebooks, but from judges, defendants, colleagues, and the unpredictable pulse of the courtroom itself.

The courtroom is a living organism—breathing through the murmurs of spectators, shifting under the weight of testimony, and at times crackling with an invisible tension that only those attuned to its rhythms can feel.

I learned that lesson early—on my very first jury trial. Unlike the many bench trials I had handled—quick proceedings over charges like prostitution, drug possession, or minor assaults—this would be different.

Three months into my rookie year, I stood in front of a jury (six jurors—the rule for misdemeanors). Presiding over it all was Judge Bruce M. Wright, known among the legal community and law enforcement alike as "Cut 'Em Loose Bruce." Feared by some and revered by others, he stood at the center of a perpetual tug-of-war between public safety and civil rights, his rulings often sparking as much outrage as admiration.

Judge Wright was an erudite African American gentleman, a poet and an author, as much at home in the literary salons of Harlem as he was behind the bench. He was also a lightning rod for controversy. His commitment to bail reform and his critiques of systemic racial injustice earned him the nickname—often uttered with derision by police officers who viewed his rulings with suspicion. But to others, including many in the Black community, Wright represented a courageous check on a deeply flawed system.

My case was relatively straightforward on paper: a charge of petit larceny—the theft of a small item by a habitual shoplifter. But beneath the surface ran dangerous currents. There were clear racial overtones to the case—biases evident in the testimony of the store security agent, perhaps even in the police conduct. I knew it. And more importantly, Judge Wright knew it.

I did my best to navigate the trial with fairness and sensitivity, careful never to exploit the tensions or ignore them. The jury ultimately convicted the defendant of petit larceny. After the verdict, I asked Judge Wright—cautiously—how I'd done. He regarded me for a moment, the lines around his eyes deepening, then smiled slightly.

"You did well," he said.

"You saw what was there. You treated it with respect."

It was a small exchange, but it stayed with me. Almost half a century later, the criminal justice system continues to confront many of the same challenges Judge Wright sought to highlight. Questions about the impact of socioeconomic status and race on outcomes persist. Yet, the neighborhoods suffering most from crime often include those most harmed by the system itself. The effort to balance justice, deterrence, and compassion is not simple. In his own way, Judge Wright did all he could to remind those paying attention that even routine cases can carry the weight of larger truths. His example—equal parts controversial and courageous—challenged prosecutors like me to consider not only what the law permitted, but also what justice demanded.

From that first trial forward, I understood that my role was never just about winning—it was about seeing and understanding.

Of course, trial work was only a part of courtroom life for a young Assistant District Attorney.

Much of it revolved around arraignments—the first formal appearance a defendant made after arrest. In the early 1980s, in order to reduce 72-hour arrest-to-arraignment delays, the Office launched a 24-hour arraignment initiative.

Junior ADAs were often assigned to the 4:00 p.m.–midnight or midnight–8:00 a.m. shifts—standing in bustling, fluorescent-lit courtrooms, processing a steady stream of humanity: pickpockets, drunks, drug dealers, prostitutes, and the occasional more serious offender.

It was grueling and, in its own way, exhilarating.

I honed my Chinatown ritual for my night arraignments: friends, and sometimes dates, came to watch the spectacle unfold. After a few hours of observing the churn of justice, we would walk to nearby Chinatown for noodles before returning to court to finish the shift.

It became a strange kind of rite of passage—for them and for me.

ECAB was another cornerstone of ADA life. It was where the process truly began—where police officers brought in freshly arrested defendants and prosecutors decided whether to file formal charges. The work required quick thinking, sharp instincts, and an ability to sift through chaos for truth.

It was in ECAB that one very memorable incident of my early career occurred.

Early in 1980, my officemate Chris Chang and I were both on shift when Bo Dietl—one of the NYPD's most notable street cops—brought in a case. Bo was a legend in his own way. A brash, hard-charging detective from the NYPD's Street Crime Unit, he made headlines for hundreds of arrests, many involving violent crimes and illegal weapons.

But his unit also had a reputation for aggressive practices, and the DA's Office had begun scrutinizing their stops and searches.

On this particular night, Chris reviewed Bo's paperwork and found problems with the stop.

He told Bo he was "DP'ing the case"—declining prosecution.

Bo exploded. In a flash, he was in Chris's face, calling him a "Chung King m-----f-----"—a racist slur that echoed across the crowded ECAB office.

Officers and ADAs quickly pulled them apart. But the incident's retelling shot like lightning up the chain of command. Robert Morgenthau himself got involved, personally calling the Police Commissioner. There were discussions about whether Bo would be fired.

In the end, he wasn't—and Bo would go on to build a colorful career in public life, running unsuccessfully for Congress, founding a security firm, and later serving on Donald Trump's Homeland Security Advisory Council.

But for me, the episode was an early and vivid lesson:

Doing right was never limited to prosecuting criminals. It meant confronting potential abuses wherever they appeared—and accepting that resistance would come with it.

Not all the headlines I touched were grim.

One improbable case catapulted me into the glare of New York's tabloid press for the first time.

It involved Mark Gastineau and Ken O'Brien—two rising stars of the New York Jets. Charismatic, swaggering, beloved by fans.

In the early morning hours at the legendary Studio 54, amid the pulsing music and its accompanying light show, a scuffle broke out—fueled, reportedly, by a drunken arm-wrestling contest gone wrong. The result was a brawl that left a bartender and several patrons injured, and two NFL players facing misdemeanor assault charges.

The case became a front-page tabloid sensation.

Studio 54 was no ordinary nightclub. It was the epicenter of celebrity culture—a nightly parade of models, rock stars, politicians, and socialites—and its every scandal drew media attention. Suddenly, I found myself at the center of it.

The trial lasted four weeks—at that time, the longest misdemeanor trial ever conducted in Manhattan. Photographers camped outside the courthouse. Reporters hounded witnesses. Every twist and turn played out in the Daily News and the New York Post.

For me, it was a baptism by fire—managing not just the legal complexities of the case, but the public glare and media criticism that came with it.

In the end, the jury convicted defensive end Mark Gastineau of assault but acquitted quarterback Ken O'Brien. Justice had been served—but so too had the realization that the intersection of law, fame, and media would become an increasingly fraught part of American public life.

It was a small case in the grand scheme of things. A misdemeanor. But it taught me something vital: in the courtroom, there are no small cases—only opportunities to stand for the idea that the rules apply to everyone, no matter how bright the lights are outside.

The boy from Valley Stream was growing up—one case, one late-night arraignment, one confrontation at a time.

The battles ahead would only grow bigger.

Chapter 5
Family Growth and Office Advancements

The years following my early trials in Manhattan were anything but quiet. I was no longer just learning the ropes; I was now trusted with homicides—summoned in the dead of night to scenes that would etch themselves into memory—and handling cases with far higher stakes than the barroom assaults and pickpocket trials that had once consumed my days. While my professional life was accelerating, my personal life was about to take an equally significant turn.

It was Valentine's Day night, 1979, when I made the decision to head uptown from my Washington Street apartment in the West Village. I had no particular plans, but my roommate, Vinnie, and I decided to make an Upper East Side outing. The neighborhood was then the city's social epicenter—bustling, polished, and, for me, inconveniently far from home. I didn't know it at the time, but this uncharacteristic deviation would become one of the most fateful nights of my life.

We stopped first at Maxwell's Plum, a famous singles bar of the era, and then made our way to a less well-known neighborhood spot called The Mad Hatter, near New York Hospital. It was small, lively, and loud enough that conversation required leaning in. I had never been to The Mad Hatter before.

There, I met Teresa—or "T," as she was known to everyone. We struck up a conversation. Numbers were exchanged. And in that time, long before texting or social media, a phone number was a promise—a reason to hope the next day might be different. She was Italian, from Seaford on Long Island's South Shore, and had been a cheerleader at Seaford High School, where she'd watched wrestling matches between our two schools. I was instantly drawn to her warmth and intelligence. She was then a dietetic intern at

New York Hospital, and The Mad Hatter was her neighborhood bar.

Before long, our lives became intertwined in more permanent ways. In late 1979, we moved in together, settling into a four-family Victorian home I had purchased in Kensington, Brooklyn. The decision seemed eccentric at the time; my friends joked that I'd fallen off the island. But something about Brooklyn's grit and potential appealed to me. I sensed that its time would come—and it did. Property values soon climbed, and the house proved to be not only a home but a sound investment. T and I moved in together and married in 1986. We lived in that house for more than a decade, rented it out for another, and eventually sold the property in 2000, which allowed us to purchase a home in the Hamptons—our summer retreat to this day.

Our daughter, Danielle, was born in the summer of 1988. We were hoping for an auspicious 8/8/88 birthday, but she decided to arrive on her own terms—on the 19th. In a moment T doesn't let me forget, on 8/8, I traveled down to Washington, D.C., to film an episode of America's Most Wanted, featuring two Westies gang members we were pursuing. By 1990, we had moved to Briarcliff Manor in Westchester County, just before I left the DA's Office. Our twins, Jake and Drew, were born in 1992 (more on these events later).

The kids are all grown now. Drew is married to Morgan, and Jake is married to Genesis. In October 2024, we experienced one of the greatest joys of our lives when Drew and Morgan welcomed our first grandchild, a boy named Shai. These milestones—though told out of order—trace the quiet architecture of my life: the foundation beneath the turbulence of my work.

But before the days of late-night feedings, there was a blur of courtroom battles, of chasing convictions and chasing sleep. Yet amid the chaos, home was always an anchor—a reminder that the pursuit of justice meant little if it didn't lead to a life worth protecting.

At the beginning of those family milestones, while T was entering my life, I was moving through the ranks in the DA's Office. I was promoted to Felony Assistant and then to Homicide Assistant and ultimately held the concurrent titles of Senior Trial Counsel and Senior Investigative Counsel—positions that carried greater responsibility and a new rhythm of work. One such rhythm was being "on call," a 24-hour stretch during which I'd be summoned to homicide scenes all over Manhattan.

On one unforgettable Christmas Day, I picked up four separate homicides. That was the reality of the job: you didn't just leave a crime scene and instantly become a husband or father again. You brought the silence of the dead home with you. I remember sitting at family dinners, physically present but mentally still standing in a bloodied hallway in Harlem, trying to bridge the gap between the violence I had just seen and the normalcy of the life I was trying to build. It took a toll that you didn't notice in the moment—a slow accretion of shadows that T had to live with as much as I did.

These were the years when New York City teetered on the edge of being ungovernable. In 1984 alone, more than 1,450 homicides were recorded—a grim number that would reach a crescendo of more than 2100 in 1990. The contrast to today's crime levels is stark: annual homicides in New York now hover in the low hundreds. But back then, violent crime was an ambient presence—part of the city's atmosphere. Crack cocaine had begun its deadly march through communities, gang violence surged, and fear was a fact of daily life. Working in the Manhattan DA's Office during that period wasn't just about enforcing the law—it was like standing at the eye of a storm, charged with imposing order where chaos reigned.

In those years, I learned that justice was rarely absolute. It lived in the gray zones—between what happened and what could be proven, between compassion and consequence. The work was relentless, but so was the belief that somewhere within the violence and exhaustion, there remained the possibility of doing right.

Among the cases that shaped my DA years, a number stood

out above the rest. Each one revealed something not just about crime, but about people—their choices, frailties, and the fine line between survival and destruction.

Chapter 6
Echoes of Murder, Inc.

There are cases that never quite leave you. They don't make headlines or shift policy, but they mark a boundary—between the part of your life where you think you understand human cruelty and the part where you realize you never will. The murder of Linda Vig was one of those cases.

Linda came to New York from Michigan full of promise—young, bright, and determined to make her own way. Instead, she became entangled with three men: Barry Shapiro, Louis Rachles, and Arthur Goldstein. They fancied themselves a kind of family, bound by a volatile mix of loyalty, drugs, and fear. Their world was small, intense, and self-contained—until Linda tried to step out of it.

We later heard from the cooperators that they claimed their criminal lineage stretched back generations, to the ghosts of Murder, Inc. That discovery gave the case a chilling dimension: it wasn't just another homicide—it was an echo from a darker era.

Murder, Inc. had been the enforcement arm of the mafia in the 1930s and early '40s, made up largely of Jewish and Italian gunmen from Brownsville and the Lower East Side. They operated out of candy stores and backrooms, killing on contract for the major syndicates. Its most infamous members—Abe "Kid Twist" Reles, Harry "Pittsburgh Phil" Strauss, Allie "Tic Toc" Tannenbaum—were part of a mythology I'd grown up hearing about in New York. When Reles turned informant, and Thomas Dewey's prosecutions dismantled the enterprise, the city exhaled—but not all its poisons drained away. By the time I was in the DA's Office decades later, I could still feel its residue in certain corners of Brooklyn. Barry and Arthur, it turned out, were descendants of men who had once worked for the original Murder, Inc. Their crimes were smaller, but the impulse—to dominate, to silence—was the same.

Linda's relationship with them was complicated. She had been romantically involved with Barry, and her presence in their apartment had become a source of tension. Whether she was killed because she knew too much, or because her independence threatened their control, would later become a question for the jury. But long before we had a case, we had silence—and silence, in its own way, can be a form of violence.

The silence broke with a single act of conscience. Barry's wife, Ellen Shapiro, came forward. Her reasons were human, not heroic. She had once resented Linda—but resentment gave way to something stronger. She told us what she knew: that Linda had been murdered in Rachles' apartment, and that her husband, along with Goldstein and Rachles were directly responsible. She knew because she had witnessed the bludgeoning of Linda. I remember thinking, as she spoke, that truth often comes not from the righteous, but from the conflicted—people torn between guilt, fear, and the need to unburden themselves.

Her account opened the door to Arthur Goldstein, who agreed to cooperate. His story was brutal. Linda had been beaten over the course of several days in Rachles' Upper East Side apartment—just blocks from the Mad Hatter, the bar where I'd met T years earlier, in what now felt like a different lifetime.

Goldstein told us that after Linda died, they placed her body in a trunk and dumped it off the coast of Brooklyn. Barry, already incarcerated for another crime, had orchestrated it all. Then Arthur revealed something we hadn't known—that Barry had previously killed an antique dealer who had refused him a loan. Linda had allegedly known about it, and that knowledge sealed her fate.

We started the case thinking we were chasing one murder. Now we were looking at two.

Two detectives from Manhattan North Homicide, Dennis Roberts and Jerry Walsh, brought me the file. They were the kind of investigators who made you believe in the profession—smart, relentless, unflinching. With Arthur's information, we obtained a search warrant for Rachles' apartment and went straight to the spot Goldstein said Linda had lain bleeding.

We pulled up the carpet, and there, in the padding beneath it, it was: brown, dried pools of blood caught in the cups of waffled foam. I remember that moment vividly—the mix of elation and nausea. This was what truth looked like when you found it too late.

Linda's body was never recovered. That absence haunted the case. Few no-body homicide prosecutions had ever succeeded in New York. But this one would. We turned to science—familial DNA, a novel concept at the time. Samples from her family in Michigan matched the blood. We had the story, the motive, and now the proof.

At Rachles' trial, both Arthur and Ellen testified. Ellen described seeing Linda's battered body in the apartment, unconscious but not yet dead. She spoke with a quiet strength that cut through the courtroom air. I had seen hardened jurors look away from gruesome photographs, but Ellen's words held them steady.

The defense tried to keep out any mention of the antique dealer's murder, arguing that it would prejudice the jury. The court disagreed, allowing it to show why Linda had to be silenced. The verdicts held on appeal. Rachles was convicted. Shapiro ultimately pled guilty. Arthur Goldstein received fifteen to life in recognition of his cooperation. All three died in prison.

For me, the case was more than a professional victory. It was a lesson in how thin the line is between loyalty and complicity—and in how truth, once it finds its way through fear, can still restore a measure of justice.

When I think about this case, I think of Linda, whose life began with hope and ended in violence. In the end, she taught me something I carried throughout my career: even the best-concealed crimes leave traces. Sometimes we find them in evidence; other times, in what people can no longer keep to themselves.

Chapter 7
The Korean Artist

Some cases live in your mind because of their cruelty. Others, because of the cost of bringing them to justice. And then there are those rare few that stay with you because of the people—because of who the victim was and what she represented. Theresa Hak Kyung Cha was one of those people. She did not just lose her life; the world lost a singular voice, and we spent years trying to give that voice its due.

Theresa was not a typical homicide victim—not in life, and not in death. She was a Korean-American artist, author, and visionary whose groundbreaking book Dictée had just been published when she was murdered on November 5, 1982. Dictée was unlike anything that had come before: fragmented, multilingual, and fearless in its confrontation with exile, colonialism, and silence. It was a meditation on identity and language, but also on how memory survives even when the body does not. In some ways, her death became the very struggle her art had foreseen—the fight against erasure.

That afternoon, Theresa had left her job at the Metropolitan Museum of Art to meet her husband, Richard Barnes, who was photographing the renovation of the Puck Building in lower Manhattan. Somewhere between her departure and their meeting point, she vanished. Hours later, her body was found in a parking lot on Elizabeth Street. She had been raped, strangled, and bludgeoned. Her pants and underwear were around her knees. Her scarf and belt were wrapped around her neck. Her distinctive wedding ring—a silver band with a black stone flanked by red ones—was gone.

The scene on Elizabeth Street told us something, but not everything. Initially, the NYPD didn't even know who she was. She was recorded in the system as an "Oriental Jane Doe." That phrase, already jarring, landed like an indictment of the times. It said everything about how the world had seen her—as invisible, anonymous, and foreign. She had spent her artistic life resisting that kind of reduction, and now, even in death, the bureaucracy was trying to return her to silence.

The investigation faltered early. Despite using a bloodhound at the Puck Building—carried down a flight of stairs by Detective Frank Donnelly—the police failed to locate where the murder had occurred. A second stairwell had gone unnoticed. It was an oversight that could have destroyed the case before it began. In those moments, when procedure fails, you realize how fragile justice really is—how dependent it is on ordinary human attention. But then, something unexplainable happened.

Theresa's brother, John Cha, had flown in from California. The family wanted to visit the building, and I gave permission. John descended that second stairwell, into a secluded part of the basement and stopped at a column marked with the number six. His mother, back home, had described the number in a dream. There, next to that concrete pillar, he found the true crime scene: blood, a red leather jacket, her gloves, her hat. Everything.

I've never been a man inclined to mysticism, but that moment unsettled me. There are times in this work when logic and faith intersect—when something beyond our own determination seems to intervene. I've learned not to question it, only to respect it.

That discovery changed the case—and forged a bond between the Cha family and me that would last through the three trials that followed.

The case fell to Detectives Marty Davin of Manhattan South Homicide and Paul Pace of the Fifth Precinct, who brought the case at its inception to me. They weren't just colleagues; they were friends. When I married T, Marty and Paul and their wives occupied four of the sixteen seats reserved for detectives and their spouses. These were not just the people I worked beside—they were the ones who understood what this work took to do, and what it took out of us, and did it anyway.

Once the crime scene was found, it did not take long to home in on the murderer. His name was Joey Sanza—also known as Anthony Gianelli—a security guard at the Puck Building, who had not returned to work after the day of the homicide, and had not been seen since. His record reflected a long and violent history. After fleeing New York, he was arrested in Florida for unrelated crimes and eventually pleaded guilty there to a dozen sexual assaults. Each attack followed the same chilling pattern: a sudden approach, a weapon, a beating concentrated on the victim's head, and a stolen ring. They were his trophies, his way of collecting proof of power.

Sanza was extradited to New York and indicted for Theresa's murder and rape. We tried him for the first time in 1984. The evidence was largely circumstantial: his flight, his actions after returning home to his roommates. But there was no eyewitness, no DNA. But we believed we had something stronger than chance—a pattern. The Florida assaults mirrored Theresa's killing with uncanny precision. We introduced those prior crimes under the legal doctrine known in New York State as Molineux, which allows evidence of prior bad acts to establish identity or modus operandi.

The jury convicted. Sanza was sentenced to twenty-five years to life for murder and another eight and a third to twenty-five for rape.

But justice, as I would learn again and again, is fragile.

The Appellate Division reversed the conviction. In People v. Sanza, 121 A.D.2d 89 (1st Dep't 1986), the court found that the Florida assaults were too prejudicial. The similarities, they said, were not distinctive enough. The conviction was vacated. It's hard to describe the feeling of watching justice unravel, not because of doubt, but because of doctrine. The law demands fairness even for the guilty—and yet, in moments like that, fairness can feel like failure.

We prepared for a second trial. The evidence was the same, but without the Florida testimony about the rings; the jury hung—one holdout. For the Cha family, it was another wound. For me, it was a lesson in endurance. There's a moment in every long case when belief becomes the only thing that keeps you upright.

Before the third trial, Marty and I went back to the beginning. We reinterviewed everyone. Marty revisited Sanza's sister and her roommate—both had noticed him acting strangely after the murder and had testified at both of the trials. Then came the break. Marty found Sanza's ex-girlfriend, Lil, now married to a well-known New York architect. She didn't want to get involved. She had rebuilt her life. But eventually, when we met her in her husband's office, she told us about a conversation she'd had with Joey. After the murder, he called her and said, "I really fucked up this time. I'm heading to Florida." It wasn't a full confession in the legal sense—but we believed it was enough to fill the gap that existed in at least one juror's mind.

Lil agreed to testify.

The third trial began in 1987. We put everything on the table: the blood, the jacket, the timeline, and now Lil's testimony. This time, the jury convicted again. The sentence matched the first. And this time, it held.

By then, I had come to know John Cha well. I watched him carry his family's grief with a strength that was almost stoic, but beneath it was something else—a quiet defiance, the same refusal to let his sister be forgotten that defined her art. Years later, he wrote The Rite of Truth, a book about Theresa, memory, and justice. Reading it, I recognized our own struggle inside his words—the courtroom as its own kind of ritual, where we summon the dead not to resurrect them, but to affirm that their lives mattered.

What stays with me even now is not just the legal work but the human texture of it all: a family following a mother's dream into a basement; detectives chasing ghosts through stairwells; a reluctant witness stepping out of silence; and a prosecutor learning, once again, that justice may, in fact, be delayed, but contrary to the old adage, does not mean that justice was denied.

Theresa's legacy did not end in that parking lot. It lives in the pages of Dictée, in the archive at the Berkeley Art Museum, and in the memory of her family, who refused to let her become another file number. And, in some small way, it lives in me too—in the lesson that persistence against temporary failure ultimately can give way to success.

Some cases are resolved quickly. Others require perseverance and resolve. Justice for Theresa Cha fell into the latter category.

Chapter 8
Behind a Locked Door

New York in the early 1980s was a city of contradictions—elegance and decay living side by side, affluence brushing shoulders with desperation. Nowhere did that contrast feel sharper than along Riverside Drive, where grand prewar facades faced the Hudson like sentinels from a more dignified past, while inside, lives unfolded with the same quiet vulnerabilities found anywhere else in the city.

One of those lives belonged to Jesse Petchers—a forty-seven-year-old real estate heir with a gentle disposition and an open heart. He lived alone in a penthouse duplex at 33 Riverside Drive, a man of modest habits despite his wealth. His generosity was unassuming, even naïve. It was the kind of kindness that invites closeness—and, with it, risk.

Jesse had taken in his housekeeper and her two sons. They lived with him for some time, until in early November of 1982 when he asked them to leave. It was a reasonable decision, perhaps overdue. But generosity has a way of blurring boundaries, and when those boundaries are crossed, danger can hide in plain sight.

On the evening of November 10, Jesse was found dead in his apartment. His skull had been fractured by violent force. The scene showed signs of a struggle and a robbery, but there was no forced entry. Whoever killed him had not broken in. They had been let inside.

The next day, one of the housekeeper's sons walked into the 20th Precinct. He gave two written statements, both denying involvement, both riddled with inconsistencies. Bobby Clark, a seasoned detective in the precinct, warned him that he was digging himself deeper into a hole he would not be able to climb out of. After being advised of his Miranda rights and apparently understanding that the false stories were not going to fly, a full confession, reduced to writing, was made to Detective Clark.

I was on homicide call and was asked to respond to the precinct to take a videotaped statement. I again advised the defendant of his rights, including his right to remain silent and to have an attorney present. The young man indicated that he understood those rights and went on to again confess his killing of the man who had given him shelter. This time the confession was on video, preserved for a jury to judge for themselves whether there was anything untoward about the treatment of the defendant, or the veracity of his statement.

I had taken scores of confessions under similar circumstances. What initially unsettled me in such interviews was the ordinary calm with which many of the defendants could speak about the taking of a life, and the seemingly cathartic nature of the confession itself. From everything I could glean at the time, this confession was exactly that.

I prosecuted the case. I had taken the statement, understood its weight, and saw the matter through to trial. The defense objected to my dual role, arguing that having the same prosecutor both take and later introduce the confession was unfairly prejudicial. They moved to suppress the statement and even requested that another prosecutor deliver the summation. The court denied both motions.

The Court found there was nothing improper about the interview—no coercion, no coaching, no pressure. And I believed, without reservation, that the defendant was telling the truth about an act he committed and could not undo.

The trial itself was quiet, almost unnervingly so. No theatrics. No drama. Just a methodical presentation of evidence. The jury watched the tape, heard the confession, and saw photographs of Jesse's shattered skull. It was a case rooted in betrayal of the most intimate kind—the kind that requires access, trust, and proximity to succeed.

Looking back, what I remember about the case is not its

complexity, but its apparent simplicity. A murder. A confession. A conviction.

There was no media frenzy. Jesse's name barely appeared in the papers. No politics, no cause célèbre—just the steady machinery of the courtroom. The jury convicted. The appellate courts affirmed.

I had a rule in my years as a prosecutor: I would never prosecute a case unless I was absolutely certain of guilt in my own mind. That rule became a form of moral armor—a way to live with the enormous power entrusted to me. In the Petchers case, I had no doubt.

Decades passed. My own life changed many times over. Then, in 2023—forty-one years after the trial—I received an email I never expected. At the time, I was serving as the Independent Consent Decree Monitor in Aurora, Colorado, overseeing a police department struggling to rebuild public trust. The message arrived through the monitorship website. It was from the defendant, long since paroled.

The email was dark and threatening in tone. Embedded within it was an assertion of innocence.

I forwarded it immediately to the Manhattan District Attorney's Office, now staffed by prosecutors young enough to be my children. By then, the Office had established a Conviction Integrity Unit—an idea I had urged years earlier, born of the belief that confidence in past convictions should never substitute for the willingness to reexamine them. The case was reviewed. I was told that nothing, in any way, suggested a wrongful conviction. I accepted that conclusion.

That should have been the end of it. But it wasn't.

The message lingered in my mind—not as an accusation, but as a reminder. It underscored a truth I had come to understand more fully over time: that the role of the prosecutor produces connections with the accused. Most of those connections are cut cleanly by verdict and sentence. Others endure.

Even in a case with no hint of misconduct, the later assertion of innocence still unsettles the conscience. It does not negate the work done or the judgment exercised at the time. But it does demand humility.

That, too, is part of doing right. Not doubting reflexively, not retreating from responsibility, but accepting that certainty in the moment does not extinguish the obligation to remain open, reflective, and accountable long after the courtroom has gone quiet. The premise would soon be tested.

Chapter 9
Blood Loyalty

When I first picked up the file of a gun possession case inherited from a colleague preparing to leave the office, I had no idea that I was stepping into the blood-soaked heart of Hell's Kitchen.

Myles Malman, a seasoned prosecutor in Trial Bureau 60, was headed south to become a federal prosecutor in Miami, where he would later prosecute and convict General Manuel Noriega, the de facto military ruler of Panama. The gun case he passed off to me—a relatively low-level felony—seemed, at the time, largely inconsequential. The defendant was already serving time on a federal gun conviction, and it was expected that he would plead guilty and receive a concurrent sentence. Yet what looked routine would become a doorway into the most vicious organized crime ring operating in New York—and, in ways I could not yet see, a thread leading to the collapse of a vicious gang known as the Westies and, ultimately, to the unraveling of the Gambino crime family itself.

The subject of the gun possession case, Jimmy Coonan, was no ordinary defendant. He led the Westies, a group known more for its savagery than for its size. And as I dug into the underlying facts of the case, I saw that this low-level weapons charge against him hinted at a larger architecture of violence. Working with detectives from the DA's Office and Manhattan South we began to examine that architecture and ultimately revealed a violent empire stretching from the alleyways of Hell's Kitchen to the neatly groomed lawns of the homes of members of the Gambino crime family.

The Westies were not your average gang. Their name alone sent shivers through anyone who had followed the headlines during the 1970s and early 1980s. They were the inheritors of a long and brutal tradition of Irish-American gangland violence in New York City. From the Gopher Gang of the early 20th century to the heyday of Owney Madden during Prohibition, Hell's Kitchen had bred a particular kind of outlaw—fierce, tribal, and deeply distrustful of authority. The Westies were the last and most violent evolution of that tradition.

Under Jimmy Coonan's leadership, the gang had transformed from street thugs into an organized, lethal enterprise. Coonan, with his steely eyes, had a reputation for being as cold-blooded as he was calculating. He rose to power by eliminating Mickey Spillane, his predecessor and one of the last so-called "gentleman gangsters," who had maintained a delicate balance between crime and community. Once Spillane was gone, Coonan filled the vacuum with blood.

Coonan's trusted enforcer, Mickey Featherstone, was a walking contradiction. A Vietnam veteran haunted by his experiences, Featherstone was known to have a volatile mix of loyalty, rage, and instability. He was both feared and pitied—a killer capable of shocking violence and someone who could, in quieter moments, show signs of deep inner torment. By the time I became involved with the group, he had already been acquitted in three homicide trials, which only added to his legend on the street. But behind that legend was a man coming undone.

By the 1960s, Hell's Kitchen occupied a space in the geography and psychology of New York City—physically adjacent to Midtown's rising skyline, yet economically and socially disconnected from its prosperity. The neighborhood's name was no affectation; it was a working-class crucible of dockworkers, longshoremen, and immigrants—mostly Irish and Puerto Rican—who lived in aging tenements and navigated a world shaped by loyalty, toughness, and not infrequently, fear. City Hall tried to rename the area "Clinton" in planning documents, hoping to sanitize its image, but to New Yorkers, it remained Hell's Kitchen—a name earned through generations of hardship and defiance.

Over the ensuing decades, the neighborhood would be transformed, though not overnight. In the '90s, as crime abated and developers turned their eyes westward, Hell's Kitchen began to shift from a zone of marginalization to one of potential. The artists and actors who had long inhabited its fringes were joined by new residents seeking affordability near the Theater District. Later, high-rise condominiums and luxury towers would begin rising along Eleventh Avenue, fueled by the larger redevelopment of Hudson Yards and Midtown's westward expansion. Even amid that change, the grit—curated or not—remained part of the story. Hell's Kitchen had not been erased—it had adapted.

But in the 1980s, crime still ruled much of daily life. You could feel the difference the moment you crossed Eighth Avenue. The air changed. The neon glow of Broadway faded into the yellow sodium vapor of streetlights that always seemed to be flickering. It smelled of diesel fumes, the Hudson River at low tide, and the stale yeast of the corner bars where Coonan held court. It was a neighborhood of shadows and hard surfaces, where outsiders were watched from the moment they stepped off the curb, and where silence was the only survival strategy worth practicing.

The economic decay of the 1970s had created a breeding ground for gangs that thrived on fear and extortion. The Westies controlled bars, construction sites, and union halls. They were known to dismember victims—a tactic chillingly referred to as "doing the Houdini." Bodies would vanish, dumped into the river or carved up so thoroughly that police had no crime scene to investigate, no evidence to pursue. No body, no case.

Their alliance with the Gambino crime family elevated their reach. The Italians had long considered the Irish too unruly to be trusted as true partners, but Coonan's brutality—and his willingness to do jobs others wouldn't—earned him a foothold in that world. The Westies became contract killers for the Gambinos.

The Gambino crime family, one of the infamous "Five Families" of the American Mafia in New York City, traced its origins to the early 20th century, but its ascent to dominance began in earnest under the leadership of Carlo Gambino in the 1950s. A cunning and soft-spoken strategist, Gambino assumed control after the assassination of Albert Anastasia in 1957 and quickly consolidated power through discretion, loyalty, and strategic alliances—particularly with the Lucchese family. Under his tenure, the Gambinos became the most powerful of the Five Families, with influence extending from the docks and construction unions to trucking, garbage hauling, and garment center rackets. Their hold on the International Longshoremen's Association helped solidify a chokehold over New York's piers—territory that overlapped with the West Side turf of the Irish-American gangs in Hell's Kitchen.

After Carlo Gambino's death in 1976, the family passed into the hands of his cousin, Paul Castellano, a businessman who emphasized white-collar crime and distanced himself from the street-level soldiers. That decision bred resentment, particularly among more violent factions led by John Gotti, who orchestrated Castellano's spectacular public assassination outside Sparks Steak House in 1985 (more on that later). Gotti's reign brought both notoriety and instability. Nicknamed the "Teflon Don" for his ability to avoid conviction, Gotti became a media darling—but his flashy style and open defiance of Mafia protocol marked a departure from Gambino's era of quiet control.

Without knowing about this hidden world of Westies–Gambino affiliation, I stepped squarely into it in a way that would prove profound when I took the Coonan weapons case. Coonan, already serving time on a separate federal gun conviction, pled out relatively quickly. But what lingered was the scent of something bigger. I followed the scent. The case opened doors—to people, to places, to patterns of behavior that had gone unnoticed or unprosecuted for years. I began working closely with a cadre of elite detectives from Manhattan South Homicide: Steve Mshar, Gene Fiocca, Jimmy Sheridan, Hugh Kelleher, Frank Donnelly, Ernie Bugge, and Joey Buffolino. These were the best of the best—tough, unrelenting, and deeply committed to rooting out evil from the streets of New York. They became not just colleagues, but friends.

The deeper we dug, the clearer it became that the Westies were more than just a violent gang. Then, in 1984, came the murder that would change everything—the killing of Michael Holly, a Westsider working on the construction of the Jacob Javits Convention Center, who knew too much and who had, weeks earlier, crossed paths with Mickey Featherstone.

Within a week of the homicide, we arrested Mickey Featherstone outside the Erie Transfer Company on West 54th Street. I still remember the geography of it: a nondescript garage in the far reaches of the West Side, not far from the Hudson River, in an area that housed the stables for the horses that pulled carriages in Central Park and its surroundings. Years later, I would live at the opposite end of that same street—a quiet, residential mirror image of the chaos that once engulfed its western sibling.

We had motive, means, opportunity, and more—we had an eyewitness who identified Mickey as the killer. The Holly murder case would ultimately become the cornerstone of the Westies' downfall. While to most, it felt like another violent death in a city that was rapidly losing its grip, we saw a different possibility. We knew we had a chance to convict Mickey Featherstone, who had evaded consequences for his prior acts of violence. But we had no idea the twists and turns the case would take and where it would ultimately lead.

As we were building our Westies case, the feds were concentrating on building cases against the Italian Mafia, or La Cosa Nostra. The Manhattan District Attorney's Office took a granular, case-by-case approach to justice. We built our cases from the street up, starting with homicides, assaults, and extortion. What we were doing with the Westies, was attempting to weave those cases into a larger fabric of organized crime. But we did not have a tool the feds did: RICO.

The Racketeer Influenced and Corrupt Organizations Act—better known as RICO—was a game-changer for federal prosecutors. Enacted in 1970, RICO allowed law enforcement to charge leaders of organized crime groups with crimes they ordered others to commit. For the first time, prosecutors didn't need to tie a mob boss directly to a specific act of violence or extortion; it was enough to show a pattern of racketeering activity conducted through a criminal enterprise. This broadened framework gave the feds a powerful tool to take down entire organizations rather than just isolated players—redefining the way complex criminal networks were investigated and dismantled.

And just a few blocks south on Centre Street, at the U.S. Attorney's Office for the Southern District, that tool was being put to good use. Rudy Giuliani, then the U.S. Attorney, was spearheading sweeping RICO prosecutions, bundling together years of criminal activity into sprawling indictments. His office had the resources, and the federal muscle to move quickly—and loudly. The FBI, too, had long prior staked its claim over organized crime investigations, and there was no love lost as we pushed forward on our own organized crime investigation.

What began as perhaps a friendly rivalry would, in time, become something far more insidious. There were law-enforcement turf wars, strategic leaks, and moments of undercutting that helped no one—not the cases, and not the city. But in these early days, it was still mostly a chess match, each side watching the other, calculating moves, and waiting to see who would make a decisive play.

For me, the Holly case was not just about one murder. It was about organized crime and exposing a network of violence, loyalty, and betrayal that had operated unchecked for far too long. I didn't yet know how deep the rabbit hole went.

But I was in it now. And there was no turning back.

Chapter 10

The Frame-Up

Despite the infighting among law enforcement, the Holly murder fell to what had effectively become the Westies Task Force—the one I was now leading. And because it was a homicide, a state-level crime rather than a federal one, it fell squarely within my jurisdiction.

By 1985, newly transferred from Trial Bureau 60 to the Office of the Special Narcotics Prosecutor at the urging of Bob Silbering, then the Chief Assistant for Special Narcotics, my team and I were at the center of the investigation that would soon extend far beyond the borders of Hell's Kitchen. The killing of Michael Holly seemed at first like another predictable act of gang vengeance. Yet what seemed like routine violence would evolve into something far more consequential, testing not only the limits of our evidence but the very integrity of the justice system itself.

The murder, on a cold night on West 34th Street, was not at first an anomaly. Holly was no innocent. He had been working construction at the Javits Center, but more notably, he was widely believed by those in Hell's Kitchen to have murdered John Bokun—an act that made him a target for revenge. He wasn't a Westie, but he was an associate who had stepped beyond the permissible lines, and that was certainly enough to get you killed in those days.

By the time of the Holly homicide, we had been investigating the Westies through narcotics violations, using the Rockefeller drug laws as leverage to flip lower-level players and build toward the murders that defined the organization. The Holly investigation supercharged our efforts. Mickey Featherstone's arrest outside the Erie Transfer Company seemed to give us the chance to have Mickey join his boss, Jimmy Coonan, in prison. And despite his record of beating cases, this time, we thought we had him.

There was a motive—revenge for Bokun's killing. There was an opportunity. And there was an eyewitness who placed Mickey at the scene. None of us—myself or the detectives Steve Mshar, Frank Donnelly, and Joey Buffolino—had any doubt. We knew Mickey's history, his volatility, his legend. The case felt airtight. Finally, the man who had lived above consequence seemed destined to face it.

But nothing about this case would turn out to be simple. During the investigation, Holly's wife, and critical background witness, was killed in a car accident upstate, but we put the case together and prepared for trial.

The trial was held in a traditional wood-paneled courtroom at 100 Centre Street, presided over by the no-nonsense Judge Alvin Schlesinger. The room was tense. Mickey sat flanked by his lawyers, who were fixtures in the Westies' orbit. Though officially independent, it was widely understood that they were the gang's house counsel.

The case was solid: eyewitness testimony, circumstantial evidence, a clear motive, and an unshakable belief in Mickey's guilt. We built our case, argued it well, and in the end, we won.

When the guilty verdict came in, I felt vindicated. After years of near misses, Mickey Featherstone—Hell's Kitchen's untouchable—was finally going to prison. The courtroom seemed to exhale. I thought justice had been served. Weeks later, Mickey was sentenced to twenty-five years to life.

And then the phone rang.

It was mid-April 1986, just weeks before my wedding. Mickey wanted to meet. He had reached out not only to me but also to the feds. He was proclaiming his innocence—not generally, but in this case. What Mickey told me, seemed fantastical: that Billy Bokun, a fellow Westie and John Bokun's brother, had deliberately dressed like Mickey the night of the murder—including a wig—to frame him. Yet, as crazy as it sounded, we had an obligation to fully understand and investigate his story.

My wedding was on May 3, 1986. My detective friends were all there, and during the reception, the talk was all about the stunning turn in the case.

When T and I left for our honeymoon, the Featherstone case was in an uneasy holding pattern. Although he had reached out, the details of a meeting with Mickey were not settled and needed to be worked out. But in 1985, there was no email, no texting, and certainly no way to monitor developments from a ship's deck.

What followed was a trip defined less by beaches and sightseeing than by logistics. I spent an unreasonable amount of time on ship-to-shore radio access and lining up at phone booths in ports of call, with collect calls to Bob Silbering, who was running point in my absence. T, who had every right to be frustrated, took it in stride. She understood that the timing of the case was out of our hands.

Those days became a small lesson in how personal milestones and professional obligations often ran on parallel tracks, intersecting whether you wanted them to or not. We helped obtain independent and non-conflicted counsel for Mickey, and by the time T and I returned to New York, the meeting with Featherstone was set. Whatever rest the honeymoon was supposed to provide had been replaced by anticipation—a recognition that the next phase of the case was about to begin.

The first meeting with Mickey took place the week after I returned, in a suite at the Sheraton Hotel in New Rochelle. It was surreal. Mickey sat across from me, Walter Mack from the U.S. Attorney's Office, and several federal agents—FBI Agents Marilyn Lucht and Art Ruffles, and Jim Nauwens, a special investigator from the Southern District. My detectives were there too: Mshar, Donnelly, Buffolino. The man we had convicted of murder was now explaining that murder to us from the other side of the table. His calm, his specificity, the growing plausibility of what he described—it all began to shift something fundamental.

He admitted to a litany of other murders, offered a roadmap to Westie operations, but swore he had nothing to do with Holly's death. It was a stunning reversal; one I didn't believe at first. But he had something more—he had a plan to prove it.

He told us about Bokun, about Kevin Kelly, about Kenneth Shannon. He named names, described the setup, and detailed where remains and other relevant evidence could be found. It was a chilling anatomy of betrayal, delivered without self-pity. But we wanted corroboration—admissions from those who had actually participated. We devised a two-pronged approach.

First, we arranged a series of monitored visits at Rikers Island, where Shannon, Kelly, and Bokun could be recorded discussing the murder and the frame-up. With help from the Department of Corrections' Inspector General, we wired the visiting room where Mickey met his visitors—and collected damning evidence.

Second, Mickey's wife, Sissy, agreed to wear a wire. Her courage was remarkable. Through her, we captured conversations that not only exonerated Mickey but revealed the full machinery of deception behind the frame.

By this time, I had been recruited to the legendary Rackets Bureau—the same unit from which Tom Dewey had once taken down Murder Inc. Mike Cherkasky, my friend and old sparring partner from the misdemeanor trial program, had become Bureau Chief in a shakeup of the Bureau. He spoke with Bob Silbering, who had recruited me to Special Narcotics just a little more than a year earlier. Mike explained that Mr. Morgenthau wanted to restore the Rackets Bureau and revive its historic mission—and with Mickey's cooperation, we now had the ammunition to do it.

I was, quite literally, traded between bureaus like a ballplayer, but I negotiated one thing: when I went to Special Narcotics, I had been designated Senior Trial Counsel. On my move to Rackets, I would receive the title Senior Investigative Counsel—the first in the office to hold both.

The recordings were everything we could have hoped for. They confirmed Mickey's story. He had been framed. The Westies' house lawyers, it turned out, had represented Mickey at trial while also representing the man who actually committed the crime.

When we had exhausted the work needed to be done with Mickey's cooperation being kept secret, I filed a motion to vacate the conviction. Laying out the facts as we now understood them, I asked the court to dismiss the charges. Mickey's conviction was overturned. He entered the Witness Protection Program under the supervision of U.S. Marshal Alfie McNeil—a legend in the world of witness security.

From that point forward, we operated as a joint federal–state task force in prosecuting the gang, with both state and federal cases being made. I was cross-designated as an Assistant United States Attorney and worked alongside the Southern District team—Mary Lee Warren, and David Brodsky. We coordinated the federal RICO prosecution with the state murder cases, although it was agreed that we would not take an active role in each other's trials. I indicted more than a half-dozen gang members, including James Coonan and his wife, Edna; Jimmy McElroy; Billy Beattie; Billy Bokun; Kevin Kelly; and Kenneth Shannon. All were ultimately convicted in both state and federal court. Kelly and Shannon fled but were caught after I appeared on America's Most Wanted. Once apprehended, they were convicted in state court, along with Bokun, for the Michael Holly homicide.

There were tensions, of course. The DA's Office and the Southern District had always had a complicated relationship—part cooperation, part competition but in this case, it worked. We shared one goal: to dismantle the Westies once and for all.

The case changed how I saw the work. It forced me to confront how fallible the system can be—that someone like Mickey Featherstone, with blood on his hands, could still be wrongfully convicted. It drove home, in a very real way, that which was instilled in new Manhattan ADAs from day one: the job is less about winning cases and more about getting them right.

In the end, the case was monumental: we brought the Westies

era to a close and helped lay the groundwork for the gentrification of Hell's Kitchen. We also set in motion the unraveling of Italian organized crime itself, including the eventual fall of John Gotti.

But it all began with a man who said, "I did a lot of things. But I didn't do this." And he was telling the truth.

Chapter 11

Turning the Knife Inward

If the first breach in the Westies' wall of silence came with Mickey Featherstone's decision to cooperate, it was James McElroy and Billy Beattie who widened the crack into a full-blown collapse.

Featherstone's dramatic post-conviction reversal shocked the gang, but it was the calculated decisions by McElroy and Beattie—both deeply embedded figures in the crew—that signaled that the Westies were no longer held together by loyalty, fear, or code. Each man made his choice under very different circumstances, at different times, and each did so for reasons that were as much personal as strategic. Beattie cooperated with the feds, but McElroy, for reasons of his own, decided not to. But their collective cooperation provided the connective tissue we needed to not only take down the core of the Westies, but to draw a straight, unbroken line to the doorstep of the Gambino crime family and its flamboyant leader, John Gotti.

These were not small-time figures. Jimmy McElroy had been Jimmy Coonan's enforcer, a man who could read a room in an instant and impose discipline with terrifying precision. Billy Beattie, for his part, had helped run the gang's day-to-day operations with a mix of discretion and ruthless calculation. Both men were implicated in the Westies' most brutal crimes and stood at the heart of the organization during its bloodiest years.

What makes their stories remarkable is not simply that they flipped—but that they did so with consequences far beyond the West Side of Manhattan. What began as a set of state homicide prosecutions evolved into a coordinated assault on organized crime itself. McElroy and Beattie, in their different ways, gave us what no indictment alone could—credibility, corroboration, and a map of a criminal ecosystem from the docks to Midtown boardrooms.

It is, in the end, a story of two men who, faced with betrayal, prison, and near-certain death, chose instead to bring the house down.

Jimmy Mac: The Enforcer Who Turned

If Mickey Featherstone was the soul of the Westies—the tormented, unpredictable warrior—then Jimmy McElroy was its spine. Broad-shouldered, heavy-handed, steeped in Hell's Kitchen's traditions, Jimmy Mac was one of the most feared men on the West Side. A boxer by training, a killer by trade, he wore the Irish mob's brutality like a second skin. He wasn't the strategist—that was Coonan—but he was loyal and relentless. For years, he never questioned and never betrayed.

Jimmy's story was literally built on blood and concrete. He grew up playing hockey in neighborhood parks and learned to fight in its gyms. By the time I came to know him, he had become a legend—the driver of the Westies' infamous meat wagon, the van used to cart dismembered remains to remote dump sites. He killed with his hands, with a gun, and with unwavering obedience to Coonan. Yet beneath that brutality was a surprising capacity for reflection, and eventually, remorse.

After Featherstone began cooperating, his disclosures pointed directly to Jimmy's role in multiple acts of violence—including the shooting of union official John O'Connor at the Gambinos' behest. We indicted, arrested, and, after he was convicted in federal court, flipped him. He would not cooperate with the feds, but he did agree to work with us.

Recognizing both the risk and value of his cooperation, the Manhattan DA's Office took the extraordinary step of assuming physical custody of him. After his federal conviction and accompanying 60-year sentence, we arranged for his transfer to state custody to face the charges we had brought against him. When he agreed to cooperate, we took him out of Rikers and put him into our own custodial witness protection program. The secure holding facility at SUNY Maritime College beneath the Throgs Neck Bridge was a spartan fortress of cinderblock, which

Jimmy ultimately shared with a cooperating witness on one of Bob Viteretti's cases. I personally negotiated the arrangement with the dean, a self-described police buff, who gave us the latitude we needed. It was far from a luxury suite. The rooms smelled of industrial cleaner and damp concrete. We sat on metal folding chairs for hours, drinking bad coffee from Styrofoam cups, while McElroy—a man who had dismembered bodies for a living—sat just feet away, his voice low and monotone, peeling back the layers of a criminal empire while the foghorns groaned in the distance.

It was there that long days of debriefing occurred for more than a year, as we moved toward bringing what some later called the case of the century. Days were spent in interviews that rewrote our understanding of the Westies' reach and their relationship to the Gambinos. On days when there were no debriefings, Jimmy took "field trips" on police launches, with a squad of detectives in tow, fishing under the bridges—a strange mix of confinement and reprieve.

Over those months, I came to know him well. He could be crude, sometimes funny, but also unexpectedly candid about the wreckage he had caused. He never asked for sympathy, and I never offered it. But there was an unspoken understanding: he wanted to help undo some of what he'd done, and we needed what only he could give.

As previewed in the Prelude, Jimmy would testify in our prosecution of John Gotti, directly linking him to the O'Connor shooting. He testified as bravely and forthrightly as he could, but the feds would not reduce his sentence. They remembered his refusal to cooperate with them and his hatred toward them. We urged leniency, but they refused. Unlike Featherstone, who entered witness protection, Jimmy was denied it. His cooperation in a state case against a mob boss, it seemed, didn't count.

He was sent back to federal custody, eventually to Lompoc, California—a long way from Tenth Avenue.

The trial record of McElroy's testimony was thick with every murder, every dismemberment, every load of body parts dumped into the Hudson, and was laid out in clinical detail. What it never contained was a single page about the boy he had been: the fatherless kid in a cold-water flat on West 47th Street, the eighth-grade dropout who could throw a perfect left hook, the teenager who believed the Westies were the only union that would ever have him. The courtroom saw the monster; the childhood that made him never came into evidence.

This, of course, was by design for the courtroom. We needed the jury to feel the weight of what he had done, not the weight of what had been done to him. But the silence around that boy still left a nagging question I have never been able to shake: if no one is willing to trace the path from that child to this killer, how will we ever be able to stop the next boy from walking it?

Years later, long after the verdict and the fireworks over Ozone Park had burned themselves out, pieces of that missing story finally surfaced. From a federal prison in Lompoc, California, diabetic and confined to a wheelchair, McElroy began exchanging letters—hundreds of them—with a young writer named Walidah Imarisha. Over seven years, she became the first person he ever allowed inside the walls he had spent a lifetime building. He spoke at length not only of his early childhood, but of his sharing of a cell with Sundiata Acoli, the Black Panther incarcerated since 1973, and how the two old men—one a white Irish killer, the other a revolutionary—somehow found a common language in the ruins of their lives. The enforcer I once debriefed under the Throgs Neck Bridge drew pencil sketches of the old Hell's Kitchen tenements and talked of the path he traveled to the witness stand and beyond. When McElroy died in 2011 at sixty-six, three thousand miles from the streets he once claimed as his, the portrait was more complete.

I think often about Jimmy Mac—not just the violence, but the contradiction. He was both product and perpetrator of a brutal era. And in the end, he did what almost none of his kind ever did: he told the truth. He stood in court and gave the system something rare—knowledge, candor, and the faintest sliver of redemption. We couldn't provide him with his freedom. But we gave him a chance to lay his sins bare, not for absolution, but for the hope of some degree of mercy in the highest of all courts.

Billy Beattie: The Reluctant Confessor

If McElroy's cooperation gave us structure, Billy Beattie gave us texture—credibility within the gang's deepest recesses. Beattie was a true Westie: brutal, loyal, and cunning. He had survived the blood years alongside Coonan and Featherstone, orchestrating extortion, loan-sharking, and murder. Where McElroy understood the mechanics, Beattie understood the pulse.

His cooperation came reluctantly. Implicated in the killing of Ruby Stein and a significant number of other homicides for which he would be facing a certain life sentence, he agreed to cooperate—first with the feds, and then with our office. He would later enter the Witness Protection Program through the FBI. But drawing the full story from him took persistence.

One of the most unforgettable moments of my career happened not in a courtroom, but in a hallway with Billy. We were walking to the Grand Jury at One Hogan Place to seek indictments against Kenneth Shannon, Kevin Kelly, and Billy Bokun for the Holly homicide. I reminded him, as I always did, that his cooperation was only as good as his honesty—total honesty—and that failing to be completely truthful would negate the deal that we had reached.

He stopped, looked at me, and asked, almost casually, "Did I tell you about the cop I killed?"

I'll never forget it. There was no bravado, no attempt at leverage. Just the flat delivery of a man pretending to remember something he had deliberately hidden from us, and something that he now realized he had better fess up to.

The victim was Robert Bonds, a twenty-seven-year-old Housing Authority police officer assigned to the South Bronx. Bonds had joined the force in 1982 and, by 1985, according to Beattie, had entangled himself with the Westies—protecting drug operations, taking payments, blurring lines. But, as Beattie explained, in the Westies' world, every favor carried a half-life. When Bonds became inconvenient—asking for more money, threatening exposure—he was marked.

Beattie detailed how he and fellow Westie Larry Patrick executed him on November 20, 1985. According to Beattie, Bonds was lured in, handcuffed, and shot four times—once in the head, multiple times in the body. His gun and shield were taken. The body was dumped in the Hudson River. Months later, when it surfaced near Pier 57, it bore the unmistakable signature of Westies enforcement: the limbs detached, not by design but by the buoyancy of decomposition against cinder blocks to which the limbs had been tied.

The case proceeded in state court. The FBI and the U.S. Attorney's Office, where the RICO case was being pursued, knew of Beattie's admission, but they kept their focus on their case. Beattie's testimony in the grand jury led to Patrick's indictment. He pled guilty to the top count of murder and served more than twenty-two years in state prison before being paroled. The case, for some reason, drew little public attention.

For those of us on the inside, the implication of the case was shattering. Bonds wasn't just another casualty. He was a cop. Our ranks had been infiltrated. His murder revealed the gang's reach and its utter contempt for boundaries—rank, badge, or oath.

Beattie's confession changed the calculus. It filled in the last blank spaces on the map of the Westies' depravity, and it reminded us how narrow the line is between law enforcement and the world it tries to contain. Without that hallway moment, we might never have known the full story—or brought Patrick to justice.

With Beattie and McElroy in the fold, and Featherstone still leading the way, we finally had the triangulated foundation to finish the job. The Westies would never recover. Nor, ultimately, would the Gambino family, whose alliance with their Irish enforcers had once seemed brilliant—and proved, in the end, to hasten their undoing.

Chapter 12

The Presage

Sometimes the significance of certain events in one's life is not immediately recognized. One such moment for me came on a cold December afternoon in 1985.

At the time, I knew little about any connection between the Westies and the Gambino crime family. But by sheer happenstance—riding with two seasoned detectives from the DA's Squad, John Gurney and Mike Cocozza—I found myself witnessing a moment that would become part of mob history. Gurney would later help plant the listening device in John Gotti's meeting place, the Ravenite Social Club in Little Italy; Cocozza was our in-house expert on organized crime.

That day, we were returning from Pleasant Avenue in East Harlem, a bastion of Italian organized crime, after pursuing a separate case. As we drove through Midtown, a call came over the radio: there had been a shooting outside Sparks Steak House on East 46th Street. Gurney found a pay phone, spoke briefly with the Intelligence Division, and learned the victims' identities. The detectives exchanged a glance—they already suspected John Gotti. We turned the car toward the scene.

One of the victims, Paul Castellano, the leader of the Gambino Crime Family, was, at the time, the central target of the federal Commission Case, a sweeping RICO prosecution that for the first time sought to dismantle the Mafia's national leadership by charging the heads of New York's Five Families as a single criminal enterprise. Castellano had been indicted as the Gambino Family's representative on the Commission, and his killing—coming just weeks before trial—removed the government's most powerful defendant but, ultimately, underscored, rather than weakened, the case's core thesis: that the Mafia's power flowed from collective governance, not from any one man.

The crime scene was chaos and had a surreal, almost theatrical quality. Police lights bounced off the wet pavement and the polished chrome of the Lincoln and illuminated the blood pooling in the gutter. The air was thick with the squawk of radios and the shouts of uniformed officers pushing back the growing crowd, but near the bodies of Castellano and the second victim, his driver, Thomas Bilotti, there was a strange, grim stillness. I remember looking at Castellano's shoes—polished, expensive leather—jutting out from under the sheet, a mundane detail that made the violence of the execution feel suddenly, shockingly real.

Both men had been shot in the head and chest as they stepped from the car. It was a military-style execution, carried out during rush hour, in public view. If Castellano's assassination marked the violent end of one era of organized crime, it also announced the beginning of another—one louder, brasher, and led by Gotti.

I remember seeing Barbara Jones at the scene. At the time, she was with the U.S. Attorney's Office for the Southern District of New York, working alongside Louie Freeh—who would later become Director of the FBI—and Walter Mack, who would go on to join me in interviewing Mickey Featherstone. Two years later, I would suggest to Mike Cherkasky that Barbara would be perfect for the vacant role of First Assistant DA at DANY. She would go on to serve with distinction and eventually become a federal judge. But that night, we were both just observers, taking in a moment that was already cementing itself into the annals of criminal history.

Castellano's death was the crescendo of months of mounting internal tension within the Gambino family. The "boss of bosses," Castellano had distanced himself from the street soldiers, preferring instead to operate like a businessman—managing construction rackets and labor unions from his Staten Island mansion. His disinterest in traditional mob life, coupled with a ban on drug dealing, alienated younger captains like Gotti, who was already violating the rule and feared retribution.

By orchestrating Castellano's murder, Gotti not only eliminated a looming threat but also catapulted himself into power. The public nature of the hit—carried out during rush hour in front of civilians and surveillance—defied Mafia tradition, which prized discretion. This was a declaration: Gotti's crew was taking over, and they didn't care who saw it.

The FBI and NYPD quickly suspected Gotti, but without direct evidence or witnesses willing to talk, the case stalled. It would take years—and ultimately the cooperation of Gotti's underboss, Sammy "The Bull" Gravano—for the truth to be presented in court. Meanwhile, Gotti reveled in his new role: tailored suits, silk ties, open defiance—his persona earned him the nickname "the Dapper Don." He beat cases in 1986 and 1987 and walked out of courtrooms with a smirk that mocked the system.

But back in 1985, none of that was visible yet. As I stood there at Sparks, I was a spectator to history. The Westies' alliance with the Gambinos had not yet been exposed, and Castellano's murder was still shrouded in confusion and rumor. I could not have known that in a few short years, I would be prosecuting Castellano's killer—the man who would become the face of American organized crime.

Looking back, that day was a pivot point, a hinge between eras—the quiet moment before the explosion, the prelude to the Gotti trial, the collapse of the Westies, and the unraveling of two criminal empires that once seemed untouchable.

Chapter 13

The Yugo

By late 1985, as our investigations into the Westies deepened. After the Castellano murder, but before the Featherstone trial, a new name had come to our attention with increasing regularity: Bosko "The Yugo" Radonjić. Though not Irish, Radonjić had emerged as an unlikely figure in the Westies organization. He was Serbian by birth, nationalist by conviction, and a calculating opportunist by trade.

Radonjić's reputation was already well known to the intelligence and organized crime divisions in New York. His roots traced back to Yugoslavia, where his father had allegedly been executed by Tito's forces for supporting the royalist Chetniks during World War II. Radonjić's anti-communist fervor brought him to the United States, where he transitioned from parking lot operator in Hell's Kitchen to anti-Tito terrorist, and eventually to mob associate. His convictions for bombings of Yugoslav targets in the Midwest had landed him in federal prison, but by the time he surfaced in our world, he seemed to be entrenched in criminal activities associated with the Westies.

At the time, we suspected—incorrectly—that he might have played some role in the Castellano shooting. What we knew with greater certainty was that Radonjić had ties to both the Westies and the Gambinos under Gotti. We certainly did not have enough to charge him, but our goal was to see whether those leads we did have could be developed into evidence which could be utilized in the Holly homicide case against Featherstone or in the Castellano murder.

We also knew that he had a weakness for attractive young women, frequented the upscale bar, Jimmy Weston's, and carried himself with the kind of arrogance that suggested he believed he was untouchable.

We were determined to pull the threads we had and see where they led.

The idea came during a brainstorming session with my detectives—Frank Donnelly, Joey Buffolino, Ronnie Stripp, and Steve Mshar. We knew Radonjić's vices: women and cocaine. So, we built a sting around both. Two undercover officers—one NYPD, one from the state's Organized Crime Task Force—were selected. Striking, sharp, and well trained, they were briefed and carefully introduced into his world.

It didn't take long. The combination of flattery, beauty, and feigned criminality did the trick. Radonjić took the bait, and after some revelry at Jimmy Weston's, the two officers encountered little resistance to a post-bar rendezvous in a suite at the Sheraton Hotel. We had wired the room and positioned ourselves to observe, listen, and wait.

What unfolded was as predictable as it was unsavory. Radonjić boasted, groped, and pulled out cocaine, offering it to his companions in a display of vulgar bravado. That was our cue. We moved in and arrested him.

We thought we had something. Here was a man who we believed was embedded in the Westies' post-Coonan operations—someone who we hoped might serve as a witness against Featherstone, Gotti and others in the Gambino orbit. We brought him in, confronted him with everything we had, and tried to turn him. He listened, nodded, even joked—but he wouldn't flip. Not then. Not ever.

Neither the case against Featherstone nor a potential case against Gotti grew stronger from that episode. Nor did it help us connect the dots between the Westies and the Gambinos. But what it did give us was clarity: cooperation would be hard to come by and would require far more leverage than we had against Radonjić at the time. His refusal to cooperate was a disappointment, but it clarified the stakes.

In the years that followed, Radonjić would resurface—sometimes at the margins of our cases, sometimes at the center of darker intrigues. He would be linked to jury tampering, Balkan war crimes, and ultimately a fugitive life that ended with his death in Belgrade in 2011.

But in that Sheraton suite, in the middle of Manhattan, we saw him clearly: a man bridging two criminal worlds—one in New York and one in Belgrade. He was unwilling to turn, unwilling to break, and willing to accept whatever consequences came with not cooperating.

In the end, although we had believed he would be carrying felony-weight narcotics, he was not; we charged the case as a misdemeanor, and processed it without fanfare, with Radonjić ultimately pleading guilty and being sentenced to time served.

Despite extensive continued investigation and repeated inquiries through future cooperating Westies, we could never make a provable case against him.

In the end, it appeared that Radonjić was more closely aligned with the Gambino crime family than with the Westies themselves. His only significant subsequent indictment came not through our cases, but years later, in federal court, where he was charged for jury tampering connected to the federal prosecution of John Gotti—a charge that was ultimately dismissed. He returned to Belgrade. He remained beyond our reach—not for lack of effort or for extradition issues, but for lack of proof.

Chapter 14
The Teflon Don

I began this book with a glimpse of where my journey would lead—with Jimmy McElroy on the witness stand and John Gotti at the defense table, the air thick with spectacle and betrayal. I have recounted how that road to the courtroom began decades earlier and miles away, on the quiet streets of Valley Stream, where I first learned the difference between right and wrong. Every lesson since—from the early trials to the violence of Hell's Kitchen—brought me to that moment, the Gotti trial, where all those ideals would be put to their hardest test.

By 1989, John Gotti had become the living embodiment of American organized crime—charismatic, immaculately dressed, and seemingly untouchable. Known to the press as the "Dapper Don" and the "Teflon Don," he had already beaten several prosecutions, including a high-profile federal RICO case and a state assault trial. Beneath the polish was a man who ruled the Gambino crime family with ruthless precision. Within law enforcement, the sense of urgency to finally bring him down was palpable.

It was at this moment that Mike Cherkasky and I, newly reunited in the Rackets Bureau, stepped into the breach. This would become the first of many significant collaborations between us. Mike believed, rightly, that together we could build large-scale, organized crime cases that mattered. The Westies' investigation had laid the groundwork, but Gotti was something altogether different—bigger, more public, and, in many ways, more consequential.

The chance came from the shooting of John F. O'Connor, the business agent of Carpenters Union Local 608, as told to us by cooperating Westie Jimmy McElroy. On May 7, 1986, at 6:40 a.m., O'Connor was shot in the lobby of a midtown Manhattan building while waiting for an elevator. He survived, but the brazen nature of the assault—four bullets to the legs and buttocks—signaled more than a labor dispute. It was, we learned, retribution. O'Connor had allegedly ordered the trashing of a restaurant, Bankers and Brokers, owned by a Gambino associate, for using non-union labor. Gotti, through intermediaries, had responded by assigning the Westies to "bust him up."

My team of detectives and I had built the Westies case, and with McElroy now cooperating, the pieces began to fall into place. Wiretaps from Gotti's headquarters—the Bergin Hunt and Fish Club in Queens—obtained by the Organized Crime Task Force (OCTF), added critical detail. McElroy told us he had met Gotti and had received the order personally from capo Anthony Ruggiero. We had our witness and corroborating tapes. Morgenthau gave us the go-ahead. Working with Barbara Ditata from OCTF and Mike Warren from our Appeals Bureau, Cherkasky and I indicted Gotti for first-degree assault and fourth-degree conspiracy. Co-defendants included Angelo Ruggiero and Anthony Tony Lee Guerrieri.

We were on our way. Little did we know what was in store.

On January 23, 1989, Gotti was arrested in SoHo, near the Ravenite Social Club. I was there to witness the moment. Joe Coffey, the legendary NYPD investigator then with OCTF, despised Gotti and made the arrest himself. He and three of my detectives—all in uniform, so no one could mistake them for rival gangsters—grabbed Gotti as he exited a coffee shop. I watched, from the safety of a marked patrol car, as Gotti, never one to concede the last word, smirked and said, "Three to one I beat this charge." Coffey, without missing a beat, shot back, "Forget it, jerkoff—get in the car."

Ruggiero was terminally ill and I arraigned him at Beekman Downtown Hospital a few blocks away from my office. Gotti's arraignment, the day after his arrest, was a spectacle which took place in an overflowing courtroom. He and Guerreri entered not-guilty pleas. We argued to the judge that Gotti should be held without bail, citing the violent nature of the charges and his demonstrated ability to operate beyond the reach of ordinary constraints. The defense, as expected, countered aggressively, citing the fact that this was an assault case, not a murder case, and, of course, that Gotti was a pillar of the community. Both defendants were ultimately released on bail pending trial. As Gotti was led back to the holding cells to be processed for release, applause broke out from the other detainees—a surreal reminder of the notoriety he carried even inside a courthouse. The stage was set for one of the most closely watched criminal trials in New York City history.

The victim, O'Connor, complicated matters. He was under investigation for labor racketeering and had been indicted in 1987 for extorting over $100,000. His own criminality made him an imperfect witness, and we decided not to call him. The defense would surprise us later by doing so themselves.

We were acutely aware of Gotti's reputation for jury tampering, especially after his 1987 RICO acquittal. Our office moved to have the jury sequestered and their names withheld. Justice Edward McLaughlin granted the motion—a rare step in state court, but a necessary one. Jurors were told their identities would remain confidential and that their safety was paramount. Detectives from NYPD's Intelligence Division were assigned to assure that safety.

Three months before the trial began, in October of 1989, the back injury I'd suffered years earlier flared. I was, again, essentially paralyzed and required immediate surgery to remove scar tissue from my earlier surgery. The timing was brutal. On the same day I became incapacitated, my one-year-old daughter, Danielle, took her first steps. T, visiting me in the hospital, felt overwhelmed until the wife of the Orthodox Jewish man with whom I was sharing my hospital room arrived with five children in tow. That, T later said, put things in perspective.

I recovered quickly and hardly missed a beat. The trial began in early January 1990 and soon became a war of attrition. The courtroom at 111 Centre Street felt like a pressure cooker, both figuratively and literally. It was packed to the walls every day, a mix of Gotti's supporters in expensive suits and the press corps in rumpled shirts. The air grew heavy and stale by mid-morning, smelling of old wood polish, wet wool, and nervous sweat. Every time the door opened, the noise from the hallway spilled in—a constant reminder that the whole city was watching—before the heavy oak doors swung shut, sealing us back into the arena with the Teflon Don.

Mike opened by describing Gotti as a man who "rules by terror and intimidation." We presented the wiretaps, the McElroy testimony, and the timeline. The tapes were imperfect—grainy, coded—but they captured Gotti giving the order to "bust him up." McElroy, serving sixty years on the federal case, told the story of how the order was given and carried out. He revealed that Joseph Schlereth, a Westie operative, had pulled the trigger.

The defense, led by Bruce Cutler and Gerald Shargel, did what they did best. They painted Gotti as a misunderstood neighborhood hero, the target of overzealous prosecutors. They attacked McElroy as a liar and murderer, trading testimony for leniency, mocked the tapes, and claimed O'Connor had countless enemies. Then they called O'Connor himself as a surprise witness. He described the shooting, said he hadn't seen the gunman, and promptly invoked the Fifth when questioned about his own crimes. It was chaos—and theater.

We believed we were in control. Behind the scenes, the FBI's Ravenite bug was recording Gotti's private reflections on our case. He thought the club was his fortress. From the upstairs apartment at 247 Mulberry Street, he held court as the Gambino boss, orchestrating business with the swagger of a man convinced he was untouchable. He had no idea the walls were betraying him.

The Ravenite was no ordinary clubhouse. Opened in 1919, it had once served Italian immigrants; by the 1950s, it was firmly under Gambino control. Its unassuming façade hid the heart of a criminal empire. Under Gotti, it became his personal stage—a place to command loyalty, strike fear, and perform the legend of the Dapper Don.

Two weeks before the trial, Mike and I met with senior FBI officials. We explained precisely what we needed from the Ravenite wire: any reference to the O'Connor assault and any sign of jury tampering. They assured us we'd be informed immediately of anything relevant.

They lied.

After four days of deliberation, on February 9, 1990, the verdict came: not guilty. Gotti smiled, straightened his tie, and accepted the applause of the gallery like a man receiving an award. Minutes later, he was on Mulberry Street, cheered as a conquering king. Television cameras broadcast the celebration, and the Teflon Don myth grew stronger.

For the Manhattan DA's Office, and for Mike and me, it was more than a loss. We had gone in believing we could pierce Gotti's armor. Instead, we walked out feeling as though we'd polished it.

We would later learn the truth: that our defeat had not been delivered solely by the jury, but by betrayal. The FBI's Ravenite recordings—those we had been promised access to—captured Gotti discussing jury tampering, implicating not only his crew but an NYPD detective named William Peist, assigned to protect our jurors. Peist, once celebrated as a hero who'd returned to duty after losing a leg in a car crash, had instead sold out his oath. He leaked jurors' home addresses to the Gambinos, enabling the very tampering we'd feared.

When the Bureau finally released the tapes in 1991, the full picture emerged. The FBI had known about the tampering during our trial and stayed silent, purportedly protecting its broader investigation at the expense of ours. What had felt like a courtroom loss became something deeper—a violation of trust between institutions sworn to the same mission.

The irony was painful. The corruption that poisoned our trial became the evidence that helped convict Gotti in federal court two years later. Our loss became their victory. But it did nothing to erase the bitterness of knowing that justice had been sacrificed to strategy.

Mike and I had built the case, fought the fight, and lost on a tainted field. The trial taught us lessons we carried for the rest of our careers—that we were not only fighting defendants, but myth, empire, and, at times, our own institutions. Still, we gave it everything we had and lived to fight another day.

Gotti is long gone. The Ravenite is shuttered, its building seized and later reborn as a retail space, with the original tiled floor its only relic. Yet, the trial and the Ravenite linger in the city's collective memory—a stop on gangster tours, a symbol of an era when Little Italy's streets pulsed with quiet menace.

For me, it endures as a reminder that the gravest perversions of justice don't always come from the streets. Sometimes they rise from within the very institutions sworn to protect it—and that is a truth we can never afford to forget.

Chapter 15

Leaving the Life

After the Gotti trial, T and I decided the time was right for a change. Danielle was approaching her second birthday, and we had moved to Briarcliff Manor with the hope of growing our family and providing more stability than the long hours and unpredictable demands of the Office could offer. Gotti had been the high-water mark of my prosecutorial career—a test of everything I had learned—but it also marked a natural point of transition.

It was June of 1990, and I was boxing up twelve years of my life. The Rackets Bureau office I'd occupied had been my command center for taking down the Westies, prosecuting Gotti, and learning what justice looked like when it worked and when it failed. Now the walls were bare except for a few tack holes where photos, diplomas, and other memorabilia had hung.

Mike Cherkasky stuck his head in the door. "You're really doing this?" he asked, knowing the answer.

"I'm really doing this."

"You'll be back," he said. "Not here, maybe. But you'll be back in this fight."

He was right, though neither of us knew how right. For now, I was walking away from the best job I'd ever had—and, at times, the most frustrating. The Gotti loss still stung, not just because we'd lost but because of how we'd lost: the FBI's betrayal, the jury tampering, the realization that sometimes the system fails not despite the people in it, but because of them.

I had a daughter now. A mortgage. A wife whose patience with ADA salaries and midnight phone calls was wearing thin. I'd proven what I could prove here. It was time to see if I could do this work differently—on my own terms, with my own firm.

But leaving meant leaving cases behind. And one, in particular, wouldn't let go.

In the mid-1980s, around the time I moved to the Rackets Bureau and was dealing with the Michael Holly homicide, I was also working on a cold case with Frank Donnelly. For the remainder of my time in the Office, I found myself tethered to the 1971 murder of Cornelia Crilley. Cornelia, a 23-year-old TWA stewardess with dreams of acting, was found naked in her Greenwich Village apartment, strangled with pantyhose tied in a chillingly unique knot, her body marked by a bite that screamed of a predator's cruelty. Her boyfriend, an NYPD officer, discovered her, casting a complicated shadow over the investigation.

Teamed with Donnelly—who was also involved in the Teresa Cha murder, as well as my Westie cases—I pored over faded reports and crime scene photos, chasing leads in a city that had moved on. The knot, a taunting signature, mocked our pre-DNA forensics, and her boyfriend's alibi left us grasping at phantoms. Each dead end felt personal, a reminder of justice's elusiveness.

The Crilley case tested me in ways the fresh cases didn't. Frank and I reviewed all of the prior interviews in the case. We had evidence—the pantyhose with its distinctive knot and the bite mark molds—but 1980s forensics couldn't unlock what they held.

I remember standing on the street where she had lived, years after the murder, trying to picture what we might have missed. I could picture her there—23 years old, dreams of acting, a whole life ahead of her. And I could picture the moment those dreams ended at the hands of someone we couldn't name.

That's what haunted me about cold cases. The victims become abstractions, case numbers, folders in a file cabinet. I didn't want Cornelia Crilley to become just another folder. But, with my departure, it seemed to be destined to be so.

Yet, decades later, in 2010, I learned that Cornelia's case had broken open, not through my hands but through colleagues with whom I had worked when I was in the Office and who had remained there for more than twenty years after I left. Steve Sarracco and Melissa Mourges used science that had finally caught up with the evidence. Forensics preserved from the crime scene and the bite mark identified the killer: Rodney Alcala, the "Dating Game Killer," a charismatic monster who'd charmed audiences on a television game show in 1978, even as he hunted women like Cornelia.

Alcala was indicted in January of 2011. His guilty plea, two years later, secured a New York sentence of 25 years to life, on top of the death sentence he had received for murders in California that he had committed. The plea closed a 40-year wound, vindicating the evidence Frank and I had safeguarded. Learning of his conviction from afar, I felt a quiet triumph—not for myself but for Cornelia, whose story had haunted me. That knot, once a taunt, became a tether to justice, proof that even cold cases can find resolution. Looking back at my involvement in the case, I saw my role—preserving, persisting—as part of a longer arc of doing right, where truth can eventually speak, even if it takes decades to be heard. In 2021, Rodney Alcala died at the age of 77 of natural causes while in custody in California. The appeals of his death sentence were abated by his death.

In a fitting symmetry, the New York case was brought under the successor to Robert Morgenthau, Cyrus Vance, my dear friend from our Rackets Bureau days, and whose election campaign in 2009, I had helped run.

Cy had left the Office before I did, and moved to Seattle, where he founded a law practice. In 1986, Cy and I were the first to bring our own computers into the Office, years before the Office would computerize. We would spend lunch and after-work hours playing Dungeons and Dragons, a popular computer game of the time, on our 1984 Macs. We also used those computers for less frivolous endeavors, using what were called dot-matrix printers to produce affidavits and warrants—all before word processing came to the rest of the Office.

As I packed my belongings in my final days in the Office, I realized it wasn't just the cases I was leaving behind. Much more importantly, it was people.

There was, of course, Mike Cherkasky, my boss and trial partner and close friend, who would stay behind for another three years until we reunited for his run for Westchester County DA against Jeanine Pirro—and for so much more after.

There was Eliot Spitzer, who had worked with me in the Rackets Bureau. Brilliant and ambitious, Eliot would go on to become Attorney General and then Governor of New York—only to fall into a public scandal that reminded me how fragile even the most luminous reputations can be.

There was Bob Viteretti, who worked in the Rackets Bureau with me and had an informant named Rocky in a case he was working, whom we housed with Jimmy McElroy at SUNY Maritime College.

Bob Silbering was another. Bob had been my first boss in the Office during my summer internship in 1977. It was he who had a hand in bringing me back to the Office and who introduced me to the detectives who would become my investigative partners and closest collaborators. It was Bob who handed me the Jimmy Coonan case when Myles Malman left for Miami. Later, Bob would become the Special Narcotics Prosecutor for New York City and, more recently, author a memoir that inspired me to write this one.

There was Jim Friel—my closest friend in Trial Bureau 60—who married Lisa Mourning, an ADA from another Trial Bureau. I still remember their wedding vividly. They would later divorce, and Jim would tragically die from untreated meningitis at just 49 years old. Jim, Chris Chang, Steve Sarracco, Neil Davidowitz, and I had played poker every Thursday night for nearly a decade. Those nights, filled with laughter, arguments over the rules, and camaraderie, were as much a part of my life in the Office as any courtroom battle.

There were reporters with whom I had become friendly and

whose paths I would cross later in life: John Miller, who doggedly covered John Gotti and our state trial, with whom I would later have a professional relationship in Los Angeles where he headed LAPD's Intelligence Division and, later, when we both served as Deputy Commissioners at NYPD. And Rich Esposito, author and former editor of New York Newsday, who would later also become a Deputy Commissioner at NYPD while I was there.

And then there were those acquaintances in the Office who never became friends, but whose names would echo much louder in history. Sonia Sotomayor, then a rising star in the Office, would ascend to the Supreme Court of the United States. Bobby Kennedy would go on to become Secretary of Health and Human Services under Trump. John F. Kennedy, Jr., whose name carried the weight of a legacy, would die in a tragic plane crash years later. In yet another twist of fate, immediately after his death, while heading the Security Services Group at Kroll, I was called upon, by a mutual friend, to secure his apartment. And then there was Andrew Cuomo, whose brief stint in the Office, served as a credential for later significant public roles. I would later assist his 2006 campaign for Attorney General with opposition research, and years later, when he was governor, and I was Chief of Staff at DANY, we would find ourselves on opposite sides of his effort to restrict the Office's authority to retain and distribute forfeiture funds.

Each of them, in their own way, was part of the fabric of the Office. Each left an impression.

On my last day, I walked out of One Hogan Place carrying two boxes of personal items and twelve years of memories. I'd stood in that building as a summer intern, prosecuted my first trial, my first murder case, and helped take down one of the most vicious criminal organizations in the city's history. It was also where I had watched John Gotti walk free despite everything we knew to be true.

I'd learned that justice isn't clean. That trying to do right doesn't guarantee the right outcome. That institutions fail, that systems need constant vigilance, and that truth is only as strong as the people willing to fight for it.

The courtroom that had once seemed like a stage for truth had turned, in the end, into a study in betrayal. What I had witnessed at Sparks, and then in court, marked not just the end of an era of mob power, but the beginning of my deeper understanding of how fragile justice can be when ambition overshadows conscience.

Those lessons would follow me everywhere I went—into the private sector, back to public service, through police departments across the country. The work wasn't ending. It was just changing form.

As I loaded the boxes into my trunk, I thought about Cornelia Crilley. About the file I was leaving behind. About the hope that someone else would pick it up someday and finish what Frank and I had worked so hard on but failed.

Twenty years later, they would. But on that day in 1990, all I knew was that I was walking away from the case, from the people, from the institution that had defined my twenties and thirties.

It was time to see if I could do this work on my own terms. Time to build something new. Time to find out what came next.

Chapter 16
Private Investigation Done Differently

As I prepared to leave the Manhattan District Attorney's Office, I found myself asking not only what would come next, but what hadn't been tried yet. I had spent years immersed in organized crime, public corruption, and complex prosecutions. But I also knew there was a need for investigative rigor outside the courtroom—one that could work with law firms serving corporations, institutions, and individuals facing serious risk. I didn't want to abandon what I had learned; I wanted to apply it differently—toward a mission that extended beyond prosecution but was meant to make the world, or at least some small part of it, a better place.

At the time, one model stood out: Kroll Associates. Founded in 1972 by Jules Kroll, a former Manhattan Assistant District Attorney, Kroll had transformed the notion of private investigation from the seedy world of marital infidelity surveillance into something methodical, professional, and often global in scope. Jules had started small, working out of an office on Third Avenue, helping companies audit fraudulent practices. He used his understanding of law enforcement to create a new kind of firm—one that hired former prosecutors, FBI agents, and police detectives to tackle white-collar crime, corruption, and misconduct. His timing had been perfect. The Foreign Corrupt Practices Act of 1977 gave rise to a whole new area of corporate compliance, and Jules was there to meet the demand.

From afar, I watched Kroll's evolution with admiration. The firm took on landmark assignments: tracing hundreds of millions of dollars looted by Ferdinand Marcos and "Baby Doc" Duvalier; investigating corruption within nonprofits like Covenant House; and helping financial institutions such as Goldman Sachs and Drexel Burnham Lambert conduct discreet, sophisticated due diligence. Jules had created a serious enterprise—and in the back of my mind, I wondered: if he could do it, why couldn't I?

So, I embarked on the path to do just that. I obtained my private investigator's license and founded Corplex, a private investigation firm, while simultaneously operating a boutique law practice beside it. To my knowledge, no one had tried that before. My idea was to offer integrated services—handling both the facts and the law—so clients could rely on a coordinated strategy rather than a patchwork of advisors.

T and I had left Brooklyn. Our first home, a four-family Victorian in the Kensington section, which I had purchased in 1979 for $64,000, had been where we started our life together, but we were ready for more space and a different pace. Danielle was eighteen months old and we knew we wanted at least one more child. We purchased a house in Briarcliff Manor, a bucolic town in northern Westchester County that offered a welcome contrast to the intense rhythm of our professional lives. When I left the Office two months later, I arranged to share office space in White Plains with a well-regarded law firm that also maintained an office in midtown Manhattan—an arrangement that allowed me to maintain my presence in the city while putting down new roots in the suburbs.

It was during this period of professional reinvention and personal transition that the Rodney King beating in Los Angeles gripped the nation. Captured on videotape in 1991, the graphic images of King—an unarmed Black man—being savagely beaten by LAPD officers triggered national outrage and laid bare deeply rooted issues of police brutality and racial injustice. The subsequent trial and acquittal of the officers in 1992 ignited the Los Angeles riots and served as a watershed moment in the national conversation about law enforcement accountability.

The echoes of that moment would reverberate for years—and in my own professional journey, they would resurface a decade later when I was called upon to help reform the Los Angeles Police Department, after the Rodney King beating and its aftermath were compounded by a scandal in the Rampart Division. The Rampart

Scandal exposed the LAPD's CRASH unit as a rogue syndicate, with officers framing innocents and stealing drugs, costing Los Angeles $125 million and overturning 106 convictions. Rodney King and Rampart were the LA version of the police corruption I encountered at the NYPD, not only with Detective Peist, but in a number of other scandals that had beset New York's Finest in the latter decades of the twentieth century.

These scandals in our nation's two largest police departments underscored the fragility of trust in law enforcement, a lesson that shaped my pursuit of justice, albeit now from the private sector. They shaped a national appetite for reform and underscored the need for external scrutiny when internal systems failed. That appetite would be renewed and amplified amid a future, unimaginable pandemic and an equally unimaginable act of brutality in the killing of George Floyd in Minneapolis in 2020.

At Corplex, I brought in as my first colleague a lieutenant from the Manhattan DA Squad—someone who understood investigative work from the inside out. Later, my law school friend Mark Speed joined me on the law-practice side, and, in 1993, we rented space in the Lincoln Building, across the street from Grand Central Terminal. We were focused initially on what I knew best: corporate fraud, internal misconduct, and public-sector corruption, but soon we took on insurance investigations and executive protection work as well.

Among the most meaningful hires I made in those formative days at Corplex was Joe Borelli, the former Chief of Detectives for the NYPD. Joe was one of the most admired and accomplished law enforcement figures in the city's history—a steady and formidable presence who had led investigations into some of New York's most infamous and consequential crimes. He rose through the ranks over a distinguished forty-year career, ultimately serving as Chief of Detectives from 1989 until his retirement in 1994.

Joe had been the public face of the NYPD during the Son of Sam investigation, receiving taunting letters from David Berkowitz and helping direct the massive task force that brought him to justice—a case that brought me back to my early days as a summer intern in the DA's Office. He led the Department through the racially explosive Howard Beach assault in which a group of white youths brutally attacked three Black men in 1986, leaving one dead and exposing deep undercurrents of racial tension in New York City. He was also responsible for the investigation of the 1988 assassination of Officer Edward Byrne, who was executed as he sat in his patrol car guarding a witness in a drug case—a crime that shocked the city and the nation and symbolized the brazen power of crack-era drug gangs.

In 2018, I would serve with Officer Byrne's brother, Larry, who was Deputy Commissioner for Legal Matters when I was Deputy Commissioner for Risk Management at the NYPD. Joe also oversaw investigations into the first World Trade Center bombing in 1993 and the tragic case of "Baby Hope," sparked by the 1991 discovery of a baby's body in a cooler along the Henry Hudson Parkway—a case that remained unsolved and haunted him long after he retired.

What Joe brought to Corplex was more than experience—he brought gravitas, integrity, and the quiet authority of someone who had seen everything and still believed in the mission. His presence marked a symbolic convergence: the traditions and discipline of law enforcement meeting the innovation and adaptability of private investigative work. Though his time with us lasted only a couple of years, Joe's impact on the firm's ethos—its standards, seriousness, and sense of purpose—was profound.

Joe Borelli passed away in May 2025 at the age of 93. He left behind a legacy defined by devotion to justice, an unflinching moral compass, and a quiet humility that commanded respect. I remain deeply grateful that our professional paths crossed in those early days of Corplex.

In those early days, we took on assignments that echoed my prosecutorial career. We traced embezzlement in construction projects, uncovered conflicts of interest in city contracting, and advised general counsel navigating criminal exposure. Word spread that we handled difficult cases discreetly and effectively. Our reputation grew not through advertising but through word-of-mouth.

Not long after I left the DA's Office, I was reminded that stepping out of public service did not mean stepping away from its pull. A few months into running my own law firm and doing investigative work through Corplex, I received a call from Tom Clifford of the DEA. Tom and I shared a connection through Frank Donnelly of the NYPD—someone I trusted implicitly from the many cases we had worked on together. Clifford was running a major money-laundering investigation with international reach: Operation Green Ice, a multi-country undercover effort targeting financial conduits used by the Cali cartel and their network of facilitators. The DEA needed someone who could play the role of an attorney in an undercover capacity—someone, as he put it, credible, steady, and comfortable navigating the blurred line between legitimate legal services and the façade of servicing criminal enterprises. Tom asked if I would do it.

The request came at a moment when I was still adjusting to the independence of private practice. I agreed to help, taking part in a series of calls and eventually a meeting to advance the undercover scenario. Clifford kept me posted on developments, and I stayed close to the phone, prepared for each incremental step these operations required. It was manageable, but it carried a constant, low-grade weight—never knowing when the next role-playing would be required—until real life intervened in a way that only real life can.

On April 14, 1992, T went into labor with our twins. We headed to White Plains Hospital, bags packed, with the familiar mix of anticipation and uncertainty that comes with every delivery. After several hours of monitoring, the staff told us to return in a few hours. We drove to a nearby restaurant—Livanos, a place we had always liked—and ordered lunch, trying to make use of the quiet before everything changed. T was uncomfortable but calm; I kept checking my watch, knowing the twins would not wait long. I also kept checking my phone messages, knowing that I was expecting a call from Tom Clifford.

When we returned to the hospital, things progressed quickly. Jake was born first, a straightforward delivery that brought an immediate sense of relief. But within minutes, it became clear that Drew was in trouble. He was breech, and the monitors suggested distress. What had begun as a controlled labor became a scramble to prepare for an emergency C-section. Twenty-eight minutes after Jake entered the world, his brother was delivered in an operating room bright with urgency.

Between consultations with doctors and checking on T's recovery, I found myself stepping into the hallway to return calls from Tom about next steps in the Green Ice matter. It was an odd duality—one of the most significant days of my family life punctuated by discussions of undercover roles, laundered funds, and meetings that needed to be scheduled or postponed. It was not lost on me how strange the contrast was. But these years were full of intersections like that, when competing obligations collided and the boundary between professional demands and personal milestones blurred.

By evening, both boys were stable, T was resting, and the immediate crisis had passed. I remember standing in the hospital room looking at the twins—one born in routine fashion, the other pulled abruptly into the world—and realizing how different my life had become since leaving the DA's Office. I was balancing a young family, a new business, and a role in an undercover federal operation—all at once. And yet it felt clear, even in that moment, that the work mattered most when it served the people closest to me. Green Ice would continue; the twins would grow; and I would keep trying to manage the demands of each role as they came.

It was also during the early days of Corplex that we encountered a new and evolving concept in the world of public accountability—monitorships, or as they were initially referred to, "Independent Private Sector Inspectors General," or IPSIGs.

Mike Cherkasky, who had stayed on at the DA's Office after

my departure, led an aggressive investigation into the Gambino crime family's grip on the garment industry. In a groundbreaking move, he decided that the most effective remedy for certain corrupt enterprises was to place them under independent oversight. Corplex was invited to submit a proposal to monitor the industry—an assignment that would have been a natural extension of the work I had done inside the DA's Office. We assembled our team, submitted our bid, and made our case.

But in another twist of fate, the job went to Kroll. I remember feeling disappointed but not discouraged. If anything, it indicated that we were beginning to be seen as a peer to a firm I had long admired. And unbeknownst to me at the time, that early competition would foreshadow the next chapter of my career—one that would see Corplex not as Kroll's rival, but as part of its future.

Kroll's monitorship in the Garment Center was no ordinary assignment. Under a memorandum of understanding with the Manhattan DA's Office, Kroll was empowered to act with nearly prosecutorial authority over select businesses. The firm conducted forensic audits, interviewed garment contractors and union reps, and monitored day-to-day operations in real time. In doing so, Kroll broke the back of the Gambino family's influence in the Garment District, creating a model for how private firms could serve quasi-public roles in complex regulatory environments. For me, it was an early example of what would become my own work years later in consent decrees and independent monitoring.

While I did not know it at the time, my path and that of Corplex would soon take an unexpected turn. Mike Cherkasky reached the same conclusion that I had reached three years earlier. Despite having the best of all jobs, it was time for him to leave the DA's Office. Our friendship had endured, and when he decided to run for District Attorney in Westchester County, he asked me to run his campaign. His opponent was Jeanine Pirro, then a relatively unknown local judge. Despite our raising significant ethical questions about her husband—questions that foreshadowed the federal tax-fraud conviction that later sent him to prison—Mike lost the race. Westchester was still a Republican county at the time, and even our best efforts couldn't shift the tide. Betsy, Mike's wife, continues to thank me to this day. She always knew there were different and more lucrative fish to fry.

Jules Kroll, who lived in Westchester and had been a significant campaign contributor, took notice of Mike's efforts and invited him to join Kroll shortly after the election. At the time, Mike and I were contemplating launching our own competing firm. I still remember his words when he told me he was joining Kroll: "Don't worry—we'll get back together." And he made good on that promise. In 1998, nine years after I founded Corplex, Kroll acquired the firm. It would come full circle—just not in the way I ever could have predicted.

In founding Corplex, I wasn't just starting a business. I was continuing a mission—one that began in the courtrooms of New York and would stretch, unexpectedly, around the world. But before I would move on to Kroll, I would become embroiled in a case of national interest involving the tragic crash of a jetliner off the shore of Long Island, and the controversy over what brought it down.

Chapter 17

Flight 800

In the late 1990s, amid Corplex's growth, one case gripped me like no other—not from the streets of New York, but from the skies over the Atlantic. On the evening of July 17, 1996, TWA Flight 800, en route from JFK Airport to Paris, exploded midair just 12 minutes after takeoff, killing all 230 passengers and crew on board. The aircraft plummeted into the waters off the coast of East Moriches, Long Island. In the immediate aftermath, the nation was gripped by speculation: mechanical failure, terrorism, or some other catastrophic cause.

Among those who believed the public was not being told the full story were James Sanders, a former police officer turned investigative journalist, and his wife, Elizabeth Sanders, a former TWA stewardess who, as a trainer of flight attendants, personally knew many of those aboard Flight 800. Deeply affected by the tragedy, Elizabeth became involved in efforts to understand what had happened. A TWA captain participating in the investigation with federal authorities, who was extremely skeptical of the government's official narrative, approached Elizabeth. He later provided the couple with small fabric samples from the aircraft's interior—samples that he believed showed signs inconsistent with the government's explanation for the crash, a fuel tank explosion.

It was through these samples that the Sanderses uncovered what they believed was the smoking gun.

They had the samples tested by a reputable laboratory, and the results showed traces of a substance consistent with military-grade explosives. James Sanders then published his findings and conclusions, alleging that Flight 800 had been downed by an errant U.S. Navy missile during a military exercise. The theory gained national attention through mainstream media long before the days of the internet and stirred public controversy, particularly among families of the victims and members of the aviation community.

Indeed, many eye-witnesses had provided statements to investigators indicating that they observed a streak of light coming from the ground to the aircraft prior to the explosion. Pierre Salinger, former White House Press Secretary under JFK, cited what he said was credible intelligence and endorsed the theory that a missile being tested by the U.S. Navy was involved in the downing of the flight. His claims, as well as the eyewitness statements, were dismissed by federal investigators.

James and Elizabeth Sanders were arrested and charged with conspiracy to receive and disseminate classified materials. They came to me for representation, and the case quickly evolved into more than just a criminal defense—it was a referendum on the transparency and integrity of the federal investigation.

Representing the Sanderses was a departure from many of the matters I had handled, but in a strange way, it felt familiar. The case brought back deeply personal memories of my own fraught experience with the FBI during the John Gotti prosecution.

In the Gotti case, Mike Cherkasky and I had been assured by the FBI that if they discovered evidence of jury tampering, they would inform us immediately. That promise was broken outright. Instead, the FBI withheld crucial information about the juror who had been bribed and the NYPD detective who had facilitated the bribery, leading to a verdict that, in my mind, not only did not reflect the evidence we had presented, but was instead the product of federal failures to honor basic ethical obligations. That episode cemented for me the realization that even the most trusted institutions are capable of deceit and deception in service of misguided ends. The betrayal by the federal government has stayed with me to this day.

It was impossible to separate that history from the Sanders case. At the center of the federal investigation into Flight 800 was James Kallstrom, the FBI's Assistant Director in charge of the New York Field Office. Kallstrom, whom I did not know personally, had risen through the ranks with a reputation for being smart, tough, and politically savvy. He became the public face of the TWA Flight 800 investigation—authoritative and confident, first attributing the crash to a bomb or missile based on eyewitness testimony, but then becoming unwavering in his assertion that the crash was not caused by a missile or any external attack, but rather by catastrophic structural failure brought about by a center fuel tank explosion due to a short circuit.

Kallstrom's narrative was echoed by the NTSB's final report, which concluded in August 2000 that the most likely cause of the explosion was a spark from a wire in the center fuel tank igniting vapors. The FBI closed its criminal investigation in 1997, asserting that no evidence of a bomb or missile strike had been found. But for many—including Sanders and his supporters—the official explanation never rang true.

As Sanderses case progressed, it became clear that the government's interest was not merely in prosecuting a technical violation. It was about silencing a voice that questioned the integrity of a high-profile investigation. In defending the Sanderses, in court documents and at news conferences, I publicly pushed back against the notion that investigative journalism could be criminalized, especially when it involved matters of public concern and potential government misconduct.

I would ultimately turn the Sanderses case over to another attorney when Kroll acquired Corplex, and my role there demanded my full-time focus on investigations and risk management. The case later ended with convictions for Elizabeth, James, and the pilot who had provided the fabric sample. Even though the convictions were for misdemeanors with no jail time, they were technically a win for the prosecution. Yet, the convictions, in my mind, left lingering questions about fairness, motive, and, of course, questions about a free press. But the larger battle—for the truth about what happened to Flight 800—remained, in many minds, unresolved.

In time, the story faded from headlines, replaced by new crises and new controversies. The official story satisfied most, but for me, the case remained a stark reminder of how narratives can be controlled, how truth can be negotiated, and how power can be protected. It underscored the importance of independence—in investigations, in journalism, and in the law.

The questions it raised and the mistrust it rekindled stayed with me. Like the unresolved tensions of the Gotti trial, Flight 800 became part of a pattern—an uneasy thread running through my professional life, tying together moments when justice and truth seemed just out of reach.

And so, even as I moved forward into my new role, the legacy of Flight 800 remained—a case that would not let go. Indeed, today, decades after I defended James Sanders against the FBI's prosecution for challenging the TWA Flight 800 crash narrative, the Navy missile theory lingers, covered in new forms of media like X by those who echo Sanderses' claims of a cover-up obscured by the NTSB's fuel tank verdict.

Chapter 18

Full Circle

By 1998, Kroll had undergone a remarkable evolution. What began in 1972 as Jules Kroll's boutique investigative firm, focused on anti-fraud audits, had, by the late 1990s, become a global player in investigations and security consulting. The firm had recently merged with The O'Gara Company, a public company, forming Kroll-O'Gara—a union that proved to be an ill-fated marriage. Though initially envisioned as a synergistic expansion, the merger soon revealed cultural and operational incompatibilities. Kroll's roots were steeped in methodical investigations and prosecutorial precision, while O'Gara started by manufacturing hearses and limousines and then moved into armored vehicles and security hardware. It was an uneasy blend of worlds, one that never entirely coalesced. Yet even amid the turbulence, Kroll continued to grow—and Corplex would become its first acquisition.

The path to that acquisition had begun years earlier, with Mike deciding to hook his star to Jules after our election loss in 1993. Mike quickly rose through Kroll's ranks to become its president. We had remained very close since the campaign, and his promise to get back together was about to be kept.

For the prior four years, Corplex had carried on its core work—internal investigations, litigation support, and executive protection. I had brought in two seasoned operatives from the military: Todd Ehrlich, a former Navy SEAL, and Dave Kervin, a Marine intelligence officer. Dave led our executive protection team and would go on to work with me for years across various assignments. Corplex had become a nimble, respected firm—still small in size, but increasingly visible through our work on public cases such as TWA Flight 800, which deepened our public profile and credibility.

Besides the Gambino Trucking/Garment Center monitorship, which Corplex had lost to Kroll and which firmly established the role of private-sector oversight, there were a number of other cases in which Kroll had been involved when I began emulating the firm through the formation of Corplex in 1990. Each had deepened my respect for the firm and made my decision to join it, when the opportunity arose, a natural one.

In 1990, Kroll investigated sexual misconduct and financial irregularities at Covenant House, a New York non-profit for homeless youth, confirming allegations against founder Father Bruce Ritter and leading to his resignation. The case further demonstrated Kroll's capacity to handle highly sensitive matters with a prosecutorial nexus, professionalism, and discretion.

Shortly thereafter, Kroll was hired by the Kuwaiti government to trace six billion dollars in hidden oil profits stolen by Saddam Hussein. The firm's forensic work uncovered secret accounts in the U.S. and Europe—a feat Jules Kroll later described on 60 Minutes as a career highlight. The assignment elevated Kroll's reputation as a pioneer in international asset recovery.

In 1992, the Russian government, under Boris Yeltsin, retained Kroll to locate fourteen billion dollars illegally moved from the Soviet Union before the 1991 coup. Despite limited cooperation from Russian authorities, Kroll's team froze assets in a Russian bank and exposed a web of illicit transactions, cementing the firm's global stature.

A year later, in a First Amendment case, attorney Floyd Abrams engaged Kroll to locate eyewitness Faraculah Arras for the defense of New York Newsday's "The Heroin Trail". Within two weeks, the firm produced the witness in Istanbul, underscoring its precision and reliability in support of high-stakes litigation.

In joining Kroll, I made the difficult decision to retire from the practice of law and turned my share of the firm over to my partner, Mark Speed. It was a necessary step to move fully into the world of corporate investigations and risk management. We relocated Corplex to Kroll's headquarters at 900 Third Avenue, placing me just steps away from Mike's and Jules's offices.

The move felt like a homecoming. Kroll had been the model I had studied since Corplex's inception, and now we were part of it. The cases grew more complex, the stakes higher, and the clients broader in scope—but the mission was unchanged: pursuing the truth with rigor, independence, and integrity.

As I settled into my new office in midtown Manhattan, I recognized that, in many ways, the journey had indeed come full circle—not just geographically, but philosophically. From the DA's Office to Corplex to Kroll, each step had been a progression of the same calling. Each chapter reaffirmed what I had learned since Valley Stream: that facts matter, that truth matters, and that doing right often requires persistence when the path forward is neither clear nor easy.

Chapter 19

Risk and Loss

When Corplex was acquired by Kroll in March of 1998, it marked not only the end of my ambitious experiment in independent investigations and risk management but also the beginning of a broader, more expansive phase of my professional life.

Shortly after joining Kroll, I was asked to help lead Kroll's expansion into the world of security by heading up a newly formed unit: the Security Services Group. It was a natural evolution of what we had already built at Corplex—an alignment of investigative discipline and operational foresight. The group included my executive protection team and was soon joined by Schiff & Associates, a firm which had built a strong reputation for physical security assessments, design, and engineering, that Kroll acquired shortly after the acquisition of Corplex. Schiff's expertise complemented Kroll's larger ambitions perfectly. While O'Gara focused on armored vehicles and hardware for high-net-worth individuals and government clients, our division concentrated on providing services for corporations and individuals—services that protected them at work, at home, and while traveling. With Gary Schiff and Brian Dusza leading the engineering side, we combined operational planning, human intelligence, and physical design in a way that few others had attempted. To that mix, I added a Technical Security Countermeasures (TSCM) team—experts who swept for listening devices and electronic intrusions in an era when corporate espionage was becoming increasingly sophisticated.

Shortly after the formation of the Security Services Group, I was called upon to assist in one of the most tragic and high-profile incidents of the decade—the death of John F. Kennedy Jr., his wife, Carolyn Bessette Kennedy, and her sister, Lauren Bessette. Their small aircraft disappeared en route to Martha's Vineyard on July 16, 1999, and the country entered a period of collective mourning.

I had known John during his time as an Assistant District

Attorney in Manhattan, though we were not close. Even in the crowded, high-energy environment of One Hogan Place, he carried a quiet gravity—a combination of humility and heritage that made him stand out. When the crash occurred, I was contacted by a mutual acquaintance from the DA's Office—someone who had been close to John—who reached out with concerns about the apartment's security and the family's privacy.

I mobilized our team immediately. Discretion was paramount. We posted personnel at the building, established a controlled perimeter to manage the throngs of media and mourners, and monitored the spontaneous memorial that formed directly across the street. For days, the site became a focal point of public grief—a living vigil of candles, photographs, and flowers. Our role was not dramatic, but it was essential: to preserve the family's dignity and safeguard the sanctity of a place that had, overnight, become both shrine and spectacle.

It was a poignant beginning to my tenure at Kroll—one that reminded me, in a deeply personal way, that the skills we brought to bear in risk management and security were not just about data, protocols, or technology. They were about people—about empathy amid loss and about protecting what remains when everything else has been taken.

That moment also crystallized what Kroll made possible. The move had allowed me to scale up the mission that had driven Corplex—to take what had once been a boutique practice and apply it globally, across disciplines and continents. And yet, the core of the work was unchanged. Whether in a courtroom, a boardroom, or on a darkened Tribeca street, the goal remained the same: to assist in bringing order to chaos, to uphold integrity, and to help in times of need.

Chapter 20

Building the Future

By mid-1999, as Kroll was still adapting to its merger with the O'Gara Company—an ultimately ill-fated union—I saw an opportunity to expand its footprint into a new and promising sector. While the Security Services Group continued to focus on executive protection and physical security assessments, it was clear that Kroll needed a revenue stream that wasn't episodic but recurring, durable, and capable of anchoring long-term growth.

That insight came from Dave Kervin and Todd Ehrlich, both of whom had joined me from Corplex. They pointed out the potential of government contracting—engagements that were sticky, in that once established, they tended to remain in place for years. Government clients offered something private-sector work rarely did: continuity, credibility, and reputational capital. It was a lesson that would stay with me throughout my career.

With that in mind, I proposed to Mike Cherkasky the creation of a Government Services Group at Kroll. Mike—always open to ideas grounded in strategy and purpose—quickly agreed. Our goal was simple but ambitious: to take what Kroll already did best—investigations, security consulting, and operational intelligence—and adapt it to the needs of federal, state, and municipal agencies across the country.

But success would depend on people. We needed leaders who had not only served in government but who were trusted by it—professionals whose reputations could open doors that contracts alone could not.

The first major hire I pursued was Bill Bratton. During his tenure as NYPD Commissioner from 1994 to 1996, he introduced CompStat and championed the "broken windows" theory of policing, leading to a dramatic reduction in crime citywide. His departure following a political clash with Mayor Rudy Giuliani had been abrupt, but his credentials were impeccable. He embodied the blend of operational insight and reformist vision that I wanted Kroll to represent. Bill had tried two private-sector roles immediately after leaving the NYPD—neither had worked out.

The opening came through his wife, Rikki Klieman, a respected legal analyst and anchor for Court TV. I had appeared regularly on the network during my Corplex years, and that professional overlap created an opportunity. In 1999, Bill joined Kroll as a senior adviser. He brought deep subject-matter expertise, media credibility, and an intuitive understanding of organizational reform. I could not have known then how instrumental he would later become in securing Kroll's appointment as Monitor in the LAPD Consent Decree—a story I will return to in a later chapter.

Not long after, I met Jerry Hauer—the first-ever director of New York City's Office of Emergency Management under Mayor Giuliani and one of the nation's foremost experts on crisis response and public health preparedness. We met through a mutual acquaintance and hit it off immediately. Jerry was mission-driven and allergic to bureaucracy. He didn't talk about problems; he solved them.

Upon joining Kroll in the fall of 1999, Jerry focused on expanding our emergency management and public health capabilities—particularly amid growing concerns over biological and chemical threats. His arrival solidified Kroll's presence in a domain that would soon prove essential. Early in 2000, Jerry began playing a pivotal role in our work with the Port Authority of New York and New Jersey, including the recruitment of John O'Neill, a former FBI counterterrorism expert, to head security at the World Trade Center.

Bill and Jerry had known each other before joining Kroll, although their recruitments were completely independent. Bringing them both aboard was a defining moment for me and a strategic victory for the firm. Despite skepticism from a few within Kroll who didn't yet see the value of expanding into government-facing work, their impact was immediate. Together, they validated the vision behind the Government Services Group and laid the foundation for some of the most consequential projects of my career.

Jerry passed away on August 11, 2023, after a long, courageous battle with cancer. Until his final days, he remained devoted to public service and preparedness, and his influence continues to shape the field of emergency management today.

We held a welcoming reception for Bill and Jerry in late 1999, and almost immediately found ourselves helping clients brace for Y2K. As the new millennium loomed, the world seemed poised on the edge of digital catastrophe. Banks were predicted to lose track of billions; planes might fall from the sky; power grids could collapse. Governments and corporations poured staggering sums into rewriting their code, racing against a clock no one could stop. When midnight struck, and the lights stayed on, Y2K became less a story of failure than one of success built on collective fear.

Our small role in that effort confirmed what Dave, Todd, and I had believed from the outset: government work wasn't just good business—it was good stewardship. The Government Services Group, buoyed by the addition of Bill and Jerry, became a turning point. It allowed us to deepen our engagement with public-sector clients, and it positioned us to guide them through the evolving landscape of national security, emergency preparedness, and infrastructure resilience.

Bill and Jerry also completed what became, for me, a core circle of trusted colleagues at Kroll—people bound not only by professionalism but by shared values of service and integrity. There was Mike Cherkasky, of course, whose promise to bring me into Kroll had set this journey in motion. Meg Reiss, formerly of the Kings County DA's Office, brought incisive judgment and a moral steadiness that made her indispensable. Jim Bucknam, calm and encyclopedic, came from the Southern District and had served as counsel to FBI Director Louis Freeh. Allen Appelbaum, another Southern District veteran, provided measured analysis and investigative depth. And Bob Viteretti, from my Rackets Bureau days, gave the place a sense of continuity that anchored me more than I realized at the time.

This Kroll clan (sans Mike—the teetotaler and consummate family man) often ended its days at Houston's, the restaurant in the Citicorp Center across from our offices at 900 Third Avenue. It became our unofficial mess hall—a place to decompress, trade war stories, and reflect on the curious blend of gravity and absurdity that defined life at Kroll. Some stories were hilarious, others heartbreaking, and many unrepeatable. But they were shared among people who had been in the trenches—who understood the stakes—and who, despite everything, still believed in the mission. They were more than colleagues. They were allies and friends, and they remain so to this day.

Chapter 21
Rampart

In the late 1990s, the Los Angeles Police Department (LAPD) was engulfed in the Rampart Scandal—one of the most far-reaching police corruption crises in American history. At its center stood the departments elite anti-gang unit, CRASH (Community Resources Against Street Hoodlums), operating out of the Rampart Division. What began as the arrest of a single officer soon revealed the anatomy of a broken system.

The scandal erupted publicly in 1999 following the arrest and cooperation of Officer Rafael Pérez, caught stealing eight pounds of cocaine from an LAPD evidence locker. Facing a lengthy prison sentence, Pérez agreed to testify against his colleagues, exposing a culture of misconduct that ultimately implicated more than seventy officers.

What Pérez described was staggering. Officers in the unit engaged in unprovoked shootings, beatings, planted evidence, made false arrests, theft, drug trafficking, and perjury. Most of the victims were young Latino and Black men—targets of a war on gangs that had quietly become a war on neighborhoods. The misconduct compromised not only the LAPD's integrity but also public confidence in policing nationwide. More than one hundred wrongful convictions were overturned, and the City of Los Angeles ultimately paid over $125 million in civil settlements.

The rot had grown from within. The CRASH unit, intended to curb gang violence, had been allowed to operate with near-total autonomy. Promotions were tied to arrest numbers. Aggression was celebrated as initiative. It was a command culture that rewarded the wrong virtues. Pérez and his peers acted with the confidence of men who believed themselves untouchable—until one act of greed forced the department to face the scope of its own corruption.

Timing magnified the damage. The LAPD was still reeling from the Rodney King beating of 1991, the 1992 riots that followed, and the erosion of public trust that never fully healed. Rampart wasn't just another scandal; it was confirmation of what many Angelenos already suspected—that the system had learned little from its past.

The U.S. Department of Justice took notice. Through its Civil Rights Division, the DOJ launched a formal investigation under 42 U.S.C. §14141, alleging a pattern or practice of constitutional violations. Section 14141—since re-codified as 34 U.S.C. §12601—was a relatively new but powerful tool. Rather than prosecute individual officers, it empowered the federal government to reform entire departments—to rewrite policy, restructure oversight, and rebuild public trust under the supervision of a federal judge.

The DOJ's findings confirmed what Pérez had illuminated: systemic failures in oversight, use of force, search-and-seizure practices, and supervision. Facing the prospect of protracted litigation, the City of Los Angeles entered into a Consent Decree with the DOJ on November 2, 2000. The decree required sweeping reforms—new investigative protocols, enhanced training, early-intervention systems to flag problematic officers, and the appointment of an Independent Monitor to oversee compliance.

The story of Rampart was not, in the end, about a handful of rogue cops. It was about institutional design—the absence of internal controls strong enough to restrain human failure. It became a national case study in how accountability can erode when agencies are left to police themselves.

During that same period, on the other side of the country, Kroll was quietly shaping its own role in the evolving architecture of public safety. Fueled by growing fears of terrorism, our Security Services Group was undertaking assignments nationwide—executive-protection operations that occasionally relied on part-time personnel, many of them drawn from the NYPD's Emergency Service Unit. These were the men and women who had spent their careers running toward danger. I admired them, and I learned from them.

Meanwhile, Jerry Hauer was expanding our public-sector footprint. Among the early preparedness contracts he secured were those with Amtrak and the Metropolitan Transportation Authority (MTA). As part of the MTA engagement, I accompanied Jerry and FDNY Chief of Department Peter J. Ganci Jr. to inspect a newly constructed train tunnel—a sobering exercise in safety and emergency planning beneath the city that never slept. It was a scene of quiet precision and shared purpose, though none of us could have foreseen how critical that expertise would soon become.

As events unfolded on both coasts—Los Angeles reckoning with Rampart, New York bracing for emerging threats—Kroll found itself at the intersection of two defining national priorities: accountability and security. The call for police reform was growing louder, even as the specter of terrorism was rising. I could not yet imagine that the two would soon converge—or the role we would play when they did.

My grandparents Jacob and Suzie, my mother Litza, and her older sister Thea in Vienna before the family's escape from Nazi Europe to Paterson, New Jersey. Much of our extended family was not so fortunate; their names survive mostly in memory and in the absence they left behind.

My mother Litza and my father Sam, circa 1944—two people shaped by very different hardships who found each other in wartime America and built a life marked by work, precision, and quiet resolve.

My mother Litza and me before my first haircut, 1954, at Sal and Vin's Barber Shop on Rockaway Avenue in Valley Stream—a neighborhood institution that, remarkably, still operates in its original location.

My sister Debby, my father Sam, and me in front of our house on Forest Road in Green Acres, Valley Stream—part of one of the federally planned "Greenbelt" communities first conceived during the Depression and completed in the early 1950s.

MAT STANDOUTS — This sextet of Long Islanders is pacing State U. at Binghamton to its best wrestling season ever. In front, from left, are Lou Candito of Bethpage, Bill Keee of East Meadow, and Barry Goldstein of West Hempstead. At rear are Wally Weller of Hicksville, Bill Spence of Syosset, and Jeff Schlanger of Valley Stream. The team is coached by Steve Erber of Huntington, a former Penn State captain.

Wrestling shaped me from junior high through high school at Valley Stream South and into my sophomore year at Binghamton, where a serious back injury ended my time on the mat. The lessons endured: how to withstand pressure, adapt quickly, and stay on offense and defense at once.

A clip of Long Island wrestlers entering the Class of '71 team at SUNY Binghamton—a snapshot from a period when discipline, competition, and endurance still defined much of how I understood myself.

New York University School of Law, in the heart of Greenwich Village—where I met Mark Speed, my future law partner, and Moshe Sukenik, one of my closest lifelong friends. At NYU's Criminal Law Clinic, I also first crossed paths with Joel Rudin, whose later work on wrongful convictions would eventually connect us again in the Anthony Broadwater case.

The Criminal Court Building and (Center Right) the side entrance to the District Attorney's Office at what was then 155 Leonard Street, later renamed One Hogan Place for Frank Hogan. Fourteen years of my life unfolded inside those walls: first as a line ADA, Senior Trial Counsel, and Senior Investigative Counsel, and decades later as Chief of Staff.

My original Manhattan District Attorney credentials and shield from my first years in the Office, alongside the shield from my return as Chief of Staff under District. Attorney Cy Vance. Two positions in the same institution, separated by decades and by a very different understanding of how it worked.

My wedding—the beginning of a partnership with Teresa ("T") that made everything that followed possible. My grandmother, Suzie, whose escape from the Nazis in 1938 made it all possible.

The Puck Building at Lafayette and Houston, where Theresa Hak Kyung Cha was murdered on November 5, 1982. Also shown is the cover of Dictée, her groundbreaking work, published just before her death. I tried her killer, Joey Sanza, three times; the third conviction stands, and he remains incarcerated.

Courtroom sketch by Ida Libby Dengrove from the 1984 Gastineau/ O'Brien misdemeanor assault trial. Gastineau was convicted; O'Brien was acquitted. I am pictured on the right.

On December 16, 1985, Paul Castellano and Tommy Bilotti were gunned down outside Sparks Steak House. The organized-crime detectives with whom I was working that day knew immediately that John Gotti had ordered the hit. We went straight to the scene and ran into Barbara Jones of the U.S. Attorney's Office for the Southern District of New York.

Mickey Featherstone, shown here as a Green Beret in Vietnam and in a later photograph, rose to become second-in-command of the Westies. Arrested outside the Erie Transfer Company, he was convicted in the Holly murder, then exonerated after our investigation uncovered the truth. After testifying in both state and federal proceedings, Mickey and his wife, Sissy, entered the federal witness protection program.

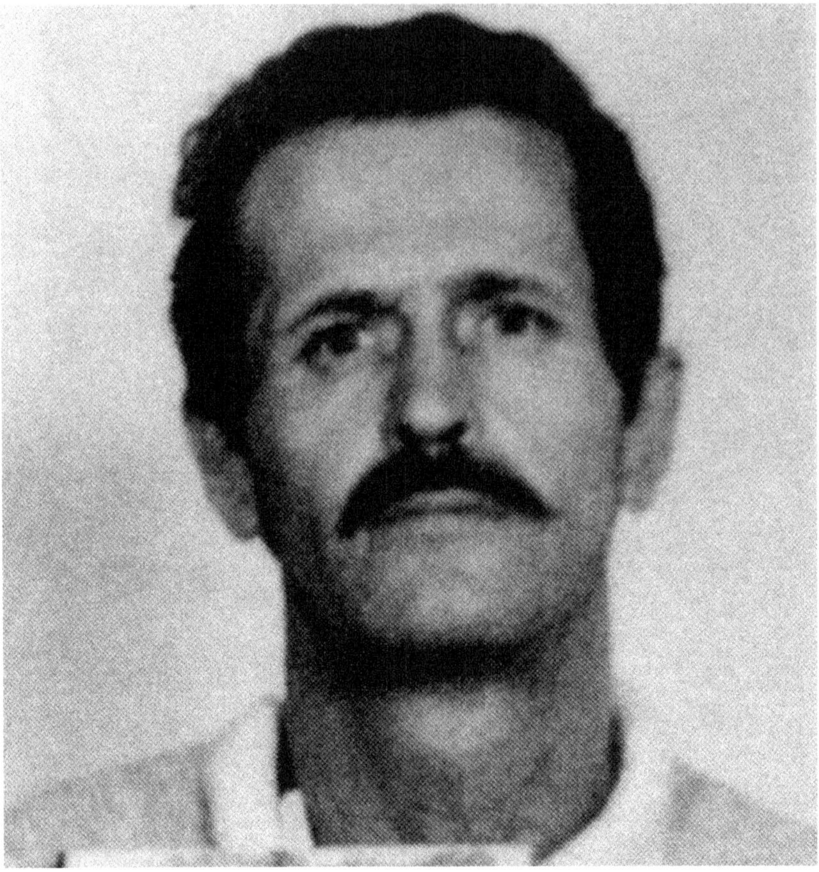

Jimmy McElroy—the man whose testimony opens this book. Once Jimmy Coonan's enforcer and one of the most feared figures in Hell's Kitchen, he took the stand in 1990 and told a jury what the Westies had done for the Gambino Crime Family. Every word seemed to cost him something; violence had long been his native tongue, and he was now trying to speak another.

John Gotti in court with Bruce Cutler and Gerald Shargel. I tried the state case with Mike Cherkasky before Judge Edward McLaughlin—the trial that opens this book. On the stand, McElroy laid out, for the first time in open court, the Westies' role as enforcement muscle for the Gambino family.

Free Press Invoked in Flight 800 Part Case

By JOHN T. McQUISTON

UNIONDALE, N.Y., Dec. 9 — The lawyer for a 52-year-old Virginia-based writer who was charged with illegal possession of pieces of the wreckage of Trans World Airlines Flight 800 tried yesterday to portray the matter as a free press issue.

The writer, James Sanders, published a book saying his investigation concluded that the plane was brought down by a missile. Yesterday, he and his wife, Elizabeth Sanders, a 51-year-old flight training supervisor for the airline, were in Federal District Court here to answer charges of illegal possession of parts of the wreckage and of withholding them from civil authorities.

Federal investigators said the Sanderses obtained the parts from a high-ranking T.W.A. pilot, Terrell Stacy, who has already admitted giving pieces of the reassembled wreckage of the plane to Mr. Sanders to help him with his book research.

The Federal charges against the Sanderses resulted from an inquiry that began in March after the Federal Bureau of Investigation learned that pieces of fabric had been removed from several seats recovered from the Atlantic after the Paris-bound Boeing 747 crashed off Long Island on July 17, 1996, killing all 230 people on board.

Mr. Sanders wrote that tests of the fabric helped confirm that a missile had caused the jetliner to explode.

The Sanderses, who surrendered today at the United States District courthouse here, appeared before Magistrate Viktor V. Pohorelsky, who released them on $50,000 bond each and ordered them to surrender their passports and to return to court on Jan. 8.

The Sanderses did not enter a plea at today's proceedings, but afterward their lawyer, Jeffrey Schlanger, said his clients denied all the charges against them.

He said that Mr. Sanders's First Amendment rights as a journalist were being violated.

Mr. Schlanger said, "The action which the Government has taken with respect to the Sanderses, in choosing to invoke a relatively new statute which was clearly intended to prevent looting of an aircraft and not situations like those at hand, is unconstitutionally chilling to the concept of a free press and certainly does nothing to alleviate the suspicions of many concerning the possibility of a Government cover-up."

The Sanderses were charged under a Federal law enacted in 1996 after a truck driver in Florida was accused of taking a piece of the wreckage of the May 1996 Valujet crash as a souvenir.

The law makes it illegal to remove, conceal or withhold parts of a civil aircraft involved in an accident. Conviction could bring a maximum of 10 years in jail, according to Ben Campbell, an assistant United States attorney.

Leaving court yesterday, Jeffrey Schlanger, the defense lawyer, held the door for his clients, Elizabeth and James Sanders.

The reconstructed fuselage of TWA Flight 800 in a National Guard hangar in Calverton, Long Island—one of the most painstaking evidence-recovery efforts in aviation history. A small strip of reddish-orange fabric recovered from this wreckage led James Sanders to challenge the government's fuel-tank explanation and eventually drew the Sanderses—and me—into the case. Shown below right are James Sanders, a former police officer turned investigative journalist, and his wife Elizabeth, a former TWA flight attendant trainer who had known many of those aboard. I represented them after their arrest, arguing that the prosecution was aimed at silencing dissent about the federal investigation.

The covers of our first and final Quarterly Reports—bookending eight years and thirty reports of oversight of the Los Angeles Police Department under the Consent Decree. What began as a response to Rampart became one of the most ambitious police-reform efforts in American history.

My Port Authority Police Department credentials, issued after I returned to New York from Los Angeles. Kroll had served as security consultant to the Port Authority, and through that relationship Jerry Hauer helped place John O'Neill—the FBI's leading expert on al-Qaeda—as head of security at the World Trade Center. O'Neill had dinner with Jerry and me on September 6, 2001, and died in the South Tower five days later. Jerry and I were deputized and asked to assist in the recovery effort.

Below Ground Zero, Silver and Gold

By JIM DWYER

About two weeks ago, a security team spotted scorch marks on a basement doorway below 4 World Trade Center, on the east side of the ruined complex, according to officials.

Even in a place of mass devastation and death, those scorch marks got fast attention. They had not been noticed by a patrol team a few hours earlier, and behind the damaged — but intact — door were nearly a thousand tons of gold and silver. To security officials, it looked as if someone had tried to break in.

Within hours, a video surveillance system was installed to keep at least an electronic eye on the precious metals until their custodian, the Bank of Nova Scotia, had a chance to remove them. That work began this week.

A team of 30 firefighters and police officers are helping to move the metals, a task that can be measured practically down to the flake but that has been rounded off at 379,036 ounces of gold and 29,942,619 ounces of silver.

There are signs of an attempt to rob a basement vault.

As layers of debris are peeled away, recovery workers are opening gangways to intact portions of a 16-acre basement that was largely unseen but was a place of spectacular scope in its own right. Just the basement area of the World Trade Center enclosed twice as much space as the entire Empire State Building.

Nearly a quarter of a mile below the spectacular vistas from the towers was their upside-down attic dropping 70 feet below the ground, a strange world with enough room for fortunes in gold and silver, for Godiva chocolates, assault weapons, old furniture, bricks of cocaine, phony taxicabs and Central Intelligence Agency files. With so many people still lost, the owners of this stuff have maintained a discreet silence during the recovery operations. But that doesn't mean they're not interested.

Beneath the Customs House — 6 World Trade Center — was an armada of government vehicles, including dozens owned by the Secret Service, in a fenced-off area. Within that area was a garage where a single armored limousine was parked under the tightest security.

The limousine was so long that it needed straight-line access to the street, because it could not clear tight corners in the basement.

That car had been used to carry heads of state visiting the city, said Tony Ball, a spokesman for the Secret Service. (The president's limousines are stored in Washington and flown everywhere he visits.)

In the 1993 trade center bombing, an armored Secret Service limousine was parked about 100 feet from a truck bomb. Although the bomb crashed through five stories of concrete and the concussion destroyed cars all over that floor, the Secret Service limousine "did not even have a broken windshield," according to a government official on the scene that

Continued on Page B11

Two Brinks trucks were at ground zero yesterday to start hauling away the $200 million in gold and silver that the Bank of Nova Scotia had stored in a vault under the trade center.

THE VAULT

Removing 1,000 Tons of Gold and Silver From Below the Rubble

Continued From Page B1

A deep pit that would gladden the heart of any criminal.

The recovery of roughly $500 million in gold and silver bullion stored in a vault beneath the World Trade Center. After the towers fell, no one knew whether the vault had survived. Kroll was retained to design and oversee the recovery, coordinating with the FDNY, NYPD, and Port Authority Police while fires still burned and the air tasted of metal. Miraculously, the vault remained intact, and the bullion was removed bar by bar.

Bill Bratton being sworn in as Chief of the Los Angeles Police Department in 2002. Three years earlier, I had recruited him to Kroll's Government Services Group; now he was leading the department we had been monitoring for more than a year.

My LAPD Monitor credentials—the physical document granting access to a department trying to rebuild itself. (This was the last renewal of our credentials. Active monitoring of the department concluded in June 2009)

In 2014, I left KeyPoint and returned to public service as Cy's Chief of Staff. Shown here are my swearing-in and, years later, Cy, Peggy, T, and me celebrating New Year's Eve in Times Square at the close of 2019.

Mayor Bill de Blasio at the podium with District Attorney Cy Vance, Police Commissioner Bill Bratton, and Deputy Commissioner Jessica Tisch at the announcement of the Mobility Initiative—a landmark collaboration through which the Manhattan DA's Office provided more than $100 million to modernize the NYPD's technology infrastructure. I spearheaded that extraordinary collaboration.

Congressman John Lewis walking me through an exhibit of his Civil Rights Movement photography at the National Center for Civil and Human Rights in Atlanta during the inaugural meeting of Prosecutors Against Gun Violence, a coalition I helped bring together to coordinate prosecutorial responses to gun violence.

Mike Cherkasky—my boss, trial partner, and friend. We met on our first day in the DA's Office in 1978 and shared many adventures over the decades. This photograph, taken in Hong Kong during the HSBC monitorship while I was still running KeyPoint, captures a later chapter in a partnership that began on Leonard Street.

NYPD
New York City Police Department

(646) 610-8515 O
(917) 863-3772 C

Jeffrey Schlanger
Counsel to the Police Commissioner

Office of the Police Commissioner
One Police Plaza, Room 1400
New York, NY 10038
Jeffrey.Schlanger@nypd.org

NYPD
New York City Police Department

(718) 610-8500 O
(718) 610-8901 F

Jeffrey Schlanger
Deputy Commissioner

Risk Management Bureau
375 Pearl Street
20th Floor, Suite 2000
New York, NY 10038
Jeffrey.Schlanger@nypd.org

My swearing-in at One Police Plaza in early 2018, administered by Police Commissioner James O'Neill (left), with First Deputy Commissioner Ben Tucker (center). I had initially joined the department as Counsel to the Commissioner before being appointed the NYPD's first-ever Deputy Commissioner for Risk Management — a newly created position reflecting the department's concern with institutional accountability.

The ribbon cutting for the NYPD Risk Management Bureau's new offices at 375 Pearl Street, November 7, 2018 — housed in the Verizon Building adjacent to One Police Plaza. The bureau's seal, visible on the glass, reflects the five stages of risk management.

My retirement from the New York City Police Department in March 2021. Between my years in the Manhattan DA's Office and the NYPD, I had given more than sixteen years of service to the City of New York—a city I had spent a career trying, in whatever ways I could, to make safer and more just.

My retired NYPD Deputy Commissioner shield and identification—the three-star rank carried by the department's most senior civilian leadership. A long way from Valley Stream.

I founded IntegrAssure in the spring of 2021, shortly after leaving the NYPD, with the goal of bringing four decades of prosecutorial and oversight experience to police departments in need of reform. Our first monitorship, overseeing the Aurora, Colorado Police and Fire Departments under a state-mandated consent decree, followed shortly after. Top: A meeting in Aurora with community leaders Reid Hettich and Omar Montgomery.

The San Leandro and Petaluma Police Departments — two California cities where I serve as Independent Police Auditor (IPA). The Office of the IPA is a permanent city entity established by statute and outsourced to IntegrAssure. From a prosecutor's office on Leonard Street to a monitor's desk in Los Angeles to independent auditor on the West Coast, the work keeps finding new form. The next chapter is still being written.

The family today — the reason this story was worth telling. From left to right: Drew, Shai, Morgan, T, me, Danielle, Genesis, and Jake. This book begins with a family fleeing annihilation in Vienna. It ends here: three generations gathered, their existence itself the answer to what survival, work, and doing right can build.

Chapter 22
Monitor

As Kroll's Government Services Group continued to take shape, the LAPD provided an unexpected opportunity—one that would alter the trajectory of both the firm and my own career.

As part of our continuing effort to expand the practice, Jerry Hauer and I took the Acela down to Washington to meet with federal officials who might make us aware of potential new work. Among our stops was a meeting with Lisa Monaco, then Chief of Staff to Attorney General Janet Reno. Lisa was sharp, direct, and quick to see potential. After hearing about our work and philosophy, she sent us to meet with Richard Jerome in the Department of Justice's Civil Rights Division.

By then, the DOJ had begun wielding its authority to confront systemic misconduct in police departments, negotiating consent decrees—court-enforced agreements requiring sweeping reform. Early test cases in Pittsburgh and Steubenville, OH, had proven that Washington could reach inside local departments and compel transformation, changing the balance of power between city halls and civil rights law.

Unbeknownst to Jerry, Bill Bratton, or me, the DOJ had just finalized such a decree with the City of Los Angeles, following the Rampart Scandal and its broader investigation into systemic issues within the LAPD. The decree required the appointment of an Independent Monitor to oversee compliance with far-reaching reforms—evaluating policy changes, tracking data, and reporting to the court. The role demanded unimpeachable credentials and credibility across every constituency: the court, DOJ, the LAPD, and the community.

The LAPD Consent Decree represented a watershed for modern policing. It was the largest and most complex federal oversight effort to date, covering one of the nation's most visible departments. From that moment forward, Los Angeles became the proving ground for what DOJ could achieve—providing a blueprint for reform that would influence consent decrees across the country for decades to come.

Our meeting with Richard Jerome turned out to be a turning point for Kroll itself. Richard—whom I would come to know well in the years ahead—was characteristically blunt. "Have you seen the RFP for the LAPD monitorship?" he asked. We had not. It had completely escaped our radar. He described the scope and importance of the monitorship, then dropped the news: the proposal was due Monday. It was Thursday.

We boarded the train back to New York in a blur of urgency. Somewhere between Baltimore and Penn Station, the stakes began to settle in. This was the kind of assignment I had been working toward for years.

Back at 900 Third Avenue, we assembled a small team—Jerry, me, and India, an extraordinarily capable intern whose energy was unbounded. With only a long weekend ahead, we drafted a proposal that captured both Kroll's institutional strength and the credibility of our people.

The structure was simple but strategic. Mike Cherkasky would serve as Primary Monitor, bringing his prosecutorial rigor, leadership experience, and deep credibility. I would serve as Primary Deputy Monitor, ensuring operational integrity and developing performance metrics. Bill Bratton would be our principal policing expert—his reform record at the NYPD spoke louder than any résumé ever could. Together, we balanced law, policy, and practice—the triad at the heart of meaningful reform.

Kroll's history in monitorships, our collective investigative experience, and the chemistry among us gave us confidence. But we also knew the field was crowded. We submitted the proposal on time—and waited.

Several months later, we were invited to Los Angeles to present our vision before a selection committee convened at City Hall. The panel included Gerry Chaleff, a respected defense attorney who would later lead LAPD's internal reform team; Barb Garrett and Ron Deaton from the Chief Legislative Analyst's Office; a representative from the City Attorney's Office; and a Deputy Chief from LAPD.

The presentation remains vivid in my memory. Mike and I outlined the operational and legal framework for oversight—how the monitor's office would function, report, and sustain independence. The room was engaged but reserved. Then Bill Bratton stood up, and everything shifted.

He spoke not from his notes but extemporaneously—about growing up in Boston, watching Dragnet on television, and the reverence he felt for Sergeant Joe Friday and his badge, number 714. "That badge," he said, "has been tarnished—not by fiction, but by reality. Our job is to help restore its shine."

For a moment, the room went still. Then came the nods.

Weeks later, the call came: Kroll had been selected as the Independent Monitor for the LAPD Consent Decree.

It was a milestone for the firm—and for me personally. Everything I had done up to that point—from prosecuting organized crime in New York to building Corplex to shaping Kroll's Government Services Group—seemed to converge in that moment. The assignment would define the next chapter of my professional life, uniting law, policy, and reform in the pursuit of something larger than any single case: the transformation of an institution once thought by some to be beyond redemption.

What began with a chance meeting in Washington and a frantic weekend of writing became one of the most consequential oversight roles in American policing. For Kroll, it was validation. For me, it was a purpose reborn.

Chapter 23
September 11

In June 2001, we made our first trip to Los Angeles to begin oversight of the Los Angeles Police Department under the Consent Decree. It was the start of a new chapter—one that would stretch across nearly a decade of monthly visits, audits, and quiet reform. During those early trips, our focus was on assembling a team, meeting stakeholders, and orienting ourselves to the city and its department.

The team we built reflected a deliberate mix of experience and temperament. Joe Buczek, a former FBI agent, brought investigative discipline. Meg Reiss brought a prosecutorial perspective. Hazel deBurgh, a Canadian accountant, offered unmatched financial and compliance rigor. Ron Filak, both attorney and CPA, served as our principal writer and analyst. Tom Frazier, former Chief of Police in Baltimore, and Harold Hurtt, former Phoenix PD Chief, were added at the DOJ's request, bringing the grounding presence of seasoned police executives. And of course, there was Bill Bratton, Mike Cherkasky, and me—each contributing a different lens on management, reform, and accountability.

We met with the Mayor, the City Attorney, union representatives, and command staff across LAPD's many divisions. We secured ID badges for Parker Center, the department's headquarters, and established our Los Angeles base at Kroll's office on 7th and Figueroa. The DASH bus stopped outside our door and dropped us at City Hall within minutes. We arranged a corporate rate at the Downtown Marriott and began settling into a routine that soon became second nature.

But second nature implies it was easy, and it wasn't. There is a jarring dislocation that happens when you spend years commuting across the continent. I would spend five days in Los Angeles being treated as the Monitor—deferred to and briefed at the highest levels—and then land back in New York to the unglamorous, necessary realities of a leaking roof or a parent-teacher conference. The re-entry was often turbulent. I missed things—small things, the kind you can't put on a schedule—and I knew that T was carrying the weight of a single parent for weeks at a time, a debt I could never quite square.

Through ride-alongs, division visits, and long conversations with officers and community members, we began to feel the scale of what we had taken on—the sheer human and institutional weight of changing a culture.

It was an intense time: nonstop travel, long meetings, and the challenge of standing up a monitorship in one of the nation's largest and most insular police departments. None of us, however, could have foreseen how abruptly the world—and the context in which we worked—was about to change.

Our fourth trip to Los Angeles was scheduled for the week of September 10, 2001. I would fly out that Monday with Mike and Bill. But just days earlier, on Thursday, September 6, Jerry Hauer and I had dinner in New York City with John O'Neill.

John had just begun his new role as Head of Security at the World Trade Center—a position Jerry, through our work with the Port Authority, which owned the World Trade Center, had helped him secure. The dinner was part check-in, part social. It was my first time meeting John. He was magnetic—sharp, funny, and fiercely committed. Over wine and conversation, he voiced concerns about the level of chatter coming from FBI and intelligence sources. There was no specific threat, he said, but something felt different. "It doesn't sound like background noise anymore," he told us.

John's reputation preceded him. Within the FBI, he had been the leading expert on al-Qaeda—instrumental in investigating the 1993 World Trade Center bombing, the African embassy attacks, and the USS Cole bombing. His conviction that Osama bin Laden posed the greatest threat to U.S. security was well known—and, to some, unwelcome. His candor and clashes with FBI leadership had forced his early retirement. His new job—protecting what he saw as the world's number one terrorist target—carried with it a bitter irony.

In the days before 9/11, John threw himself into his work, meeting with NYPD and FDNY leadership, reviewing contingency plans, and trying to mend interagency rivalries he knew could prove fatal. He had the vision, the instincts, and the urgency the moment required—but not the time.

As dinner ended, we promised to reconnect in a few weeks. That would never happen.

We arrived in Los Angeles on the evening of Monday, September 10. After checking into the Marriott, we ate at a nearby Mexican restaurant and turned in early, trying to stay on New York time. I called home, spoke with T, and went to bed unaware that the world we knew had only hours left.

I awoke at 5:30 a.m. Pacific Time, turned on CNN, and began getting ready for my workout. I called home to say good morning to T and the kids. Then the screen changed. At 5:48 a.m. Pacific Time, CNN broke into live coverage: a plane had struck the World Trade Center.

I immediately called Jerry. Given our work with the Port Authority, both of us assumed it was a tragic accident—a small plane, perhaps. But as we watched the footage, the damage was too extensive. Moments later, a second plane hit the South Tower. The silence that followed said everything. We knew this was no accident. It was war.

The rest of the day unfolded in waves of disbelief. The towers collapsed. The Pentagon was hit. Flight 93 went down in Pennsylvania. Phone lines jammed; airspace closed. Our Los Angeles office shut down as a precaution. We gathered in the hotel lobby, glued to the television, unable to look away.

For someone whose entire career had been built on

intervening—on stepping into chaos and trying to impose order—this paralyzed isolation was a specific kind of torture. I was a risk manager, yet I couldn't help protect my own city. I was a father, yet I couldn't reassure my children. Staring at that screen in Los Angeles, thousands of miles from the smoke and the fear, I felt a profound hollowing sense of uselessness that was harder to bear than the fear itself.

Then came the personal losses. Names began to surface—each one collapsing the distance between the global and the intimate. Two of our part-time employees, Paul Talty and Stephen Driscoll of the NYPD's Emergency Service Unit, were missing and presumed dead. Chief Peter Ganci of the FDNY—my companion in the recent train tunnel inspection—was gone. John O'Neill, our dinner companion only days earlier, was among the first confirmed fatalities. Meg Reiss lost the brother of her closest friend. Bill Bratton lost friends and former colleagues. Jerry knew many of the 343 firefighters who perished. The Port Authority lost 37 officers. Marsh McLennan, the company that would later acquire Kroll, lost 358 employees. My friend from Valley Stream, Jeff Goldflam, was among the more than 2,100 civilians who never came home. Thousands more would later die from the air they breathed in those days. The toll defied comprehension.

By nightfall, the enormity of what had happened began to settle. We knew the world would never return to what it had been. We also knew there would be work to do—both in the city we loved and in the country that now looked to rebuild its faith in safety, in order, and in each other.

But first, we had to find a way home. With air travel grounded and the nation paralyzed, all we could do was wait.

Chapter 24
The Return

By the end of that harrowing Tuesday, it became clear we wouldn't be getting home anytime soon. With the nation's airspace shut down and chaos unfolding by the minute, our team remained grounded in Los Angeles. We spent our days huddled in the hotel, stunned like the rest of the world. Phone calls to loved ones connected, then failed. The television images looped endlessly—smoke, collapse, dust, chaos. And beneath it all was a silence that felt almost sacred, at once urgent and paralyzing.

We waited. Wednesday passed. Thursday passed. We began checking rental car availability and preparing to drive cross-country if that became our only option. We needed to get back to our families. We needed to be in New York. On Friday morning, as we stood at the car-rental counter, word came that limited air travel was resuming, and, miraculously, we managed to secure seats on a New York flight departing from Long Beach Airport.

The airport experience was surreal. Uniformed military personnel lined the terminal, rifles in hand, eyes scanning every movement. The normal rhythms of travel—hustling passengers, busy shops, families reuniting—were gone. In their place was tension, reverence, and an almost monastic quiet. Bags were searched with an intensity we had never seen before. I remember my nail clippers being confiscated, a mundane act that suddenly carried the weight of national trauma. You could feel that the country had changed. In many ways, that morning foreshadowed the work Kroll would soon be asked to undertake—supporting the creation of the Transportation Security Administration, re-engineering airport security, and redefining what public safety would mean in this new world.

The flight itself was silent. No chatter, no laughter, no service. Just the hum of the engines and the sound of restrained breathing.

Every passenger seemed to carry an invisible burden. We were heading home, but to a home transformed by loss.

We landed to find the terminal outwardly unchanged yet utterly unfamiliar. We said goodbye with hugs and tears, then scattered to the cars and drivers who were waiting for us. The roadways, usually clogged, were nearly empty. The sky was gray; the air held a faint acrid smell. As we approached Manhattan, the hole in the skyline came into view—an absence that was not only visual but spiritual and deeply personal. Crossing through the Midtown Tunnel, past National Guardsmen with long guns checking vehicles, it was impossible to pretend the world had not turned a page.

Once back, there was little time to process. The next morning, Jerry and I were summoned to meet with officials from the Port Authority. Because of our previous work with the agency—and because Jerry had brought John O'Neill into the organization—we were viewed as trusted allies. We were officially deputized by the Port Authority Police Department. Jerry and I received PAPD windbreakers and ID cards dated 9/11/2001. I still carry mine today. This was not symbolic; it authorized us to enter secured zones, liaise with agencies, and assist in coordinating parts of the massive recovery effort.

Amid the cascading aftershocks of September 11, life resumed—but in a landscape unrecognizable. On September 29, 2001, just weeks after the attacks, our daughter was to become a Bat Mitzvah—a ceremony marking a young girl's moral and religious adulthood. It was meant to be joyous, followed by a celebration of family and music. We did not cancel the festivities, but we did tone them down substantially—forgoing flowers, donating that money to memorial causes, and placing simple baskets of apples on the tables instead. The city was grieving; so were we. We chose to move forward with a quieter spirit, one that felt respectful of the moment while still honoring her milestone.

That evening, the ceremony became more than a rite of passage; it became a moment of resilience. We honored those we had lost—John O'Neill, Jeff Goldflam, Paul Talty, Stephen Driscoll, and so many others. The reception turned into a gathering of reflection and solidarity, proof that faith and continuity could persist even when the world trembled.

A week before the Bat Mitzvah, the first major post-9/11 assignment arrived from the Bank of Nova Scotia. The bank had stored roughly $500 million in gold and silver bullion in a vault deep beneath the World Trade Center complex. After the towers fell, no one knew whether the vault had survived. Its recovery was both symbolic and logistical—a chance to reclaim stability from ruin. We were asked to lead the effort.

The site remained a disaster zone. Fires still smoldered; steel twisted like ribbons; the air was thick with dust. Our task was to design a recovery operation that could proceed without hindering rescue work or risking lives. That meant coordinating with FDNY, NYPD, the Port Authority Police Department, and engineers on site. I worked closely with Jim Spratt of the NYPD Emergency Service Unit, whose nephew would later—by coincidence—marry a cousin of mine. Together, we descended into the ruins, planning safe access to the vault.

The environment defied description. There was no financial hub in the basement—only the vault itself, sealed beneath what had once been a thriving center of commerce above. Flashlights bounced off soot-stained walls; water dripped from ruptured pipes; the air tasted metallic. Our boots crunched over debris, our voices muffled by respirators. It felt as though we were walking through the architecture of absence itself.

Miraculously, the vault was intact. The massive doors had held. Working with armored-car specialists, we organized a discreet extraction, bar by bar, each logged and verified. The symbolism was unmistakable. Amid the collapse, something had endured—a literal store of value, yes, but also a metaphor for resilience, proof that not everything precious had been lost.

Even now, I can recall the sensory overload of those days underground—the dust that clung to skin, the low rumble of machinery, the way we all moved with purpose and reverence. We weren't just recovering assets; we were bearing witness, standing at the boundary between devastation and renewal.

Two weeks after we finished the bullion recovery, tragedy struck again. On November 12, 2001, American Airlines Flight 587 crashed in the Rockaways just after takeoff from JFK. Watching the footage from my office at 900 Third Avenue, I felt the same dread I had on 9/11. Flames rose from a quiet neighborhood, homes burning, lives erased. For hours, we feared it was terrorism again. Though later ruled accidental—a result of mechanical failure and pilot response—the psychological blow was immense. New York seemed unable to catch its breath.

Even as we mourned, darker currents surfaced. The internet, still in its adolescence, began churning out conspiracy theories—many laced with antisemitism. Claims spread that Jews had been warned to stay home on 9/11, that Israel had orchestrated the attacks, and that Jewish businesses had profited from the tragedy. For those of us who were Jewish, these lies cut deeply. The city's Jewish community had suffered enormous losses. Friends, colleagues, entire families were gone. To see grief twisted into hate was to realize how fragile truth could be.

The theories metastasized, dragging in Jules Kroll and Jerry Hauer and accusing them of foreknowledge because of our work with the Port Authority. They even pointed to Maurice "Hank" Greenberg, CEO of AIG, and his son Jeffrey Greenberg of Marsh & McLennan, weaving them into grotesque fantasies about insurance and control. It was as if tragedy itself had become raw material for prejudice. Those men had lost colleagues and friends. To see their grief turned into fodder for bigots was unbearable—and prophetic of the digital disinformation age to come.

I thought of Jeff Goldflam, my childhood friend from Valley Stream, who was lost that day. Of John O'Neill, who had spent his career warning of exactly this threat. Of Paul Talty and Stephen Driscoll, my part-time employees who died trying to save others. Their memories demanded truth, not myth.

In the years since, misinformation has only multiplied. What was fringe has migrated to the center of discourse; what was unspeakable has become retweetable. The 9/11 conspiracies—especially those laced with antisemitism—linger on message boards, podcasts, and social media. They blur fact and fantasy until truth becomes just another opinion. But to those of us who lived it, who smelled the smoke, who attended the funerals, there is no ambiguity. These theories are not just false—they are profanities against memory.

9/11 shattered the city. But it also galvanized it. Amid grief came resolve. Everyone found a way to serve—donating, volunteering, helping. At Kroll, we were pressed into that service, not only because of expertise, but because of trust. We became part of New York's recovery effort, part of its moral infrastructure.

The world had changed. And so had we.

Chapter 25
Rebuilding

The months following 9/11 were among the most intense and disorienting of my career. The trauma of that day remained close, not just because of the friends and colleagues we had lost, but because we were thrust into a period of unrelenting activity. Our work with the Port Authority continued, including follow-up efforts at Ground Zero, where our team was consulted regularly on matters ranging from site security to emergency management planning. Even as the emotional fog lingered, the professional landscape shifted beneath our feet.

Across the country, priorities reset. The demand for intelligence and security surged. Kroll—positioned at the intersection of public safety, corporate security, and governmental consulting—became a natural partner in that recalibration. The company's reach began to expand not just in scope, but in philosophy. Where once we were primarily problem-solvers and risk mitigators, we were increasingly partners in institutional transformation.

Jerry was pressed into service for many of our corporate clients, navigating not only the immediate aftermath of 9/11 but also the anthrax scare that killed five people in October 2001. His profile in this area was a significant factor in his selection by Health and Human Services Secretary Tommy Thompson to stand up the Office of Public Health Emergency Preparedness, and later to serve as Director of the New York State Office of Emergency Management.

Along with an exponential increase in security work—both consulting and engineering—handled ably by Gary Schiff and Brian Dusza, the LAPD monitorship continued. Our fourth trip to Los Angeles had been interrupted by the attacks, but by the time we resumed our monthly visits, something there, too, had changed. The city felt different, and so did the work.

There was continuity in our efforts—quarterly reports, command-level interviews, systems reviews—but there was also a growing understanding that this undertaking, unlike any other we had assumed, would require significant time and patience. It was a marathon, not a sprint. The problems in Los Angeles were deep-rooted and complex, and so too was the path toward constitutional policing. What none of us could have predicted in early 2002 was that the voice whose Dragnet riff had helped win us the monitorship would soon be tapped to run the LAPD—bringing with him a force of will and a network of reformers that would reshape the engagement entirely.

By the time 2002 arrived, I was not only returning to Los Angeles each month for monitorship duties but becoming part of a larger national conversation about police reform, public safety, and resilience. Kroll, too, was evolving as the company expanded into areas that had barely existed before. The next chapter would be one of acceleration: new contracts, new domains, new alliances—still anchored in the fragile currency of trust.

In the fall of 2002, the Los Angeles Police Department was once again at an inflection point. The federal consent decree imposed in 2001, born out of the still-unfolding Rampart scandal, had begun to reshape the Department's policies and accountability systems. But leadership remained in flux. Bernard Parks, whose tenure as Chief had been defined by a rigid internal disciplinary approach and resistance to elements of the consent decree, had not been reappointed by Mayor James Hahn. An interim Chief, Martin Pomeroy, was installed, and the Police Commission, led by the president of the local NAACP, John Mack, initiated a national search for a successor.

In September, Bill Bratton approached me directly to let me know that he intended to apply for the position. Bill's reputation was already nationally burnished, having transformed the New York City Transit Police and later serving—albeit not without controversy—as NYPD Commissioner under Mayor Rudy Giuliani. His innovations, particularly the creation and implementation of CompStat, had become touchstones in modern policing. I believed then—and it proved even more true than I imagined—that his appointment would not only benefit the City of Los Angeles but would also be a critical factor in ensuring the success of the monitorship.

A few weeks later, the City of Los Angeles, recognizing Bratton's involvement on our monitoring team, reached out to me directly. They asked whether we would support their request to the Department of Justice for a waiver of any conflict of interest arising from his transition from Independent Monitor to LAPD Chief. We supported it without hesitation, and DOJ agreed.

Bratton was ultimately selected by Mayor Hahn after being recommended as one of three finalists by the Police Commission. His appointment reflected a deep desire for reform within the City and signaled a decisive break with the LAPD's insular traditions. He was only the second outsider to be named Chief in modern LAPD history. He brought with him not only a nationally respected résumé but also a proven ability to guide large urban police departments through periods of change.

On October 28, 2002, Bill Bratton was sworn in as the 54th Chief of the LAPD. I made a special trip to Los Angeles for the ceremony and sat on the dais at the Police Academy in Elysian Park. The venue itself was steeped in symbolism—the place where every LAPD officer began their journey now bore witness to the beginning of Bratton's own transformative tenure.

Mayor Hahn administered the oath. Seated among the attendees were members of the Police Commission, senior LAPD command staff, community leaders, and Bratton's wife—and my television-appearance mentor—Rikki Klieman. In his remarks, Bratton spoke directly to the moment: the need to restore trust, reduce crime, and fully embrace the reform obligations of the consent decree. He did not shy away from the Department's troubled past, nor from the enormous expectations now placed upon him. What struck me most was not only the substance of his remarks, but the ease with which he commanded the moment. This was a man who had led before. He understood what transformation was required—

and that the challenge in Los Angeles was not merely about crime statistics, but about cultural change.

In the months that followed, Bratton distinguished himself from his predecessors in both tone and strategy. His greatest strength was talent recognition—and empowerment. Among those who became part of the inner circle of reform, and with whom I developed both personal and professional relationships, were a number of remarkable individuals.

John Miller, the reporter from my Gambino days, was brought in as Bureau Chief of the Counterterrorism and Criminal Intelligence Bureau, blending journalistic instincts with strategic clarity. John Linder, another trusted Bratton advisor, helped craft messaging and strategy as the Department sought to win over both its critics and its own members. Linder and I would form a bond that ultimately brought me into the NYPD fifteen years later. From within the LAPD's ranks, leaders like Jimmy McDonnell rose quickly; he would go on to become a key operational thinker in the Department, later Chief in Long Beach, Sheriff of Los Angeles County, and, in November 2024, Chief of the LAPD. Gerry Chaleff, who had served as President of the Police Commission, joined Bratton's executive team to oversee internal compliance and risk management efforts and became my primary liaison during the term of the decree. Michael Berkow, formerly Chief of Police in nearby Irvine and known for his work on professional standards and internal affairs, emerged as a reform-driven voice on accountability.

In addition, Bratton quickly adapted CompStat for Los Angeles, expanded outreach to communities long marginalized, and restructured elements of the Department to reflect post-9/11 realities, including a significant expansion of counterterrorism functions.

But more than that, he modeled a different kind of leadership. Where Bernard Parks had emphasized discipline and control, Bratton emphasized accountability and innovation. Where Daryl Gates had resisted oversight, Bratton welcomed it. And where the

Department had once been governed by fear of change, it was now led by someone who saw change not as a threat, but as an opportunity.

His appointment marked a new chapter not only for the LAPD, but for our work as monitors. It meant that we had a leader on the inside who understood the mandate and believed in its purpose. It also meant that reform—once framed primarily as compliance—could now become a shared vision. For the City of Los Angeles, that made all the difference.

Chapter 26
Securing a Changed World

The monitorship, while a huge part of my work at Kroll, was not the only critical area in which I was involved. Among the many forward-looking efforts underway during this period was our involvement in pandemic preparedness, driven in large part by growing concerns in 2002 surrounding the avian influenza virus, commonly referred to as bird flu. Although the virus did not become a widespread public health emergency in the United States, the alarm it caused in global health circles triggered a wave of strategic planning within public safety and homeland security agencies. Jerry, always ahead of the curve and attuned to emerging threats that could destabilize public infrastructure, was particularly active during this period. Before his departure for HHS in mid-2002, he worked closely with public health officials and emergency managers to model potential scenarios, develop continuity plans, and conduct tabletop exercises designed to stress-test local and national responses to a fast-spreading, deadly virus.

Much of the work done during that period had its roots in historical memory—specifically, the 1918–1919 influenza pandemic, which had claimed tens of millions of lives worldwide. Those who studied public health understood that it was not a matter of if a new global pandemic would strike, but when. The bird flu scare acted as a wake-up call for the national security community, prompting serious conversations about supply chains, quarantine protocols, and mass-casualty contingencies. Yet, for all that was modeled and imagined in 2002, the next true pandemic would not arrive until 2020—seventeen years later.

When COVID-19 emerged, it became evident that many of the right questions had been asked in the years following bird flu, but institutional memory and political will proved fragile. Still, those early efforts offered a glimpse into the future and underscored the value of integrating public health into national security planning—

something Jerry recognized long before it became a global imperative.

Pandemic preparedness was only one part of the broader post-9/11 realignment. Another, equally consequential shift was unfolding in the domain of national security hiring. In the wake of the September 11 attacks, the machinery of the federal government began to shift into high gear. Entire new departments were created, most notably the Department of Homeland Security, and existing agencies, including Customs and Border Protection and Immigration and Customs Enforcement, were expanded rapidly. With this growth came a corresponding surge in the demand for federal workers with security clearances—individuals whose backgrounds had to be thoroughly vetted before they could be entrusted with access to sensitive or classified information.

This was not a minor uptick; it was a tidal wave of demand. Virtually every agency with national security responsibilities—Customs and Border Protection (CBP), Immigration and Customs Enforcement (ICE), the newly minted Transportation Security Administration (TSA), and others—faced backlogs that threatened their ability to function.

This backlog wasn't just a pile of paper; it was a silent crisis. Every unvetted file represented a person walking into a secure facility, boarding a ship, or sitting at a computer terminal with a badge they hadn't fully earned yet. In the post-9/11 world, that gap kept many awake at night. It wasn't just processing forms; it was closing a window of vulnerability that our adversaries were actively looking to exploit.

Traditionally, background investigations for security clearances had been conducted in-house by the Office of Personnel Management (OPM). But in 1996, in a move emblematic of the broader trend toward privatization, OPM spun off its Federal Investigative Service into a private entity—USIS (U.S. Investigations Services). Created as part of the Reinventing Government initiative under the Clinton Administration, USIS had effectively inherited the government's internal capabilities for conducting personnel security investigations. It became the dominant player in the space, controlling the vast majority of the market and operating with little competition.

By 2002, however, it was increasingly evident that USIS could not meet the exploding demand. Backlogs grew. Agency frustration mounted. For me, the opening was clear. Kroll had long been in the business of conducting background investigations—albeit in the private and corporate realm. Our clients were banks, law firms, and multinational corporations seeking due diligence on new hires, acquisitions, or executive board candidates. Security clearance work was different. It was governed by federal regulations. The protocols were stricter, the paperwork more voluminous, and the consequences of error more serious. But at its core, it was still investigative work. And I believed that with the right people, systems, and training, we could do it—and do it well.

It was a risk, no doubt. But I also saw it as an opportunity to position Kroll Government Services (KGS) in a way that aligned with the post-9/11 priorities of the country. We targeted agencies with OPM-delegated authority to run their own investigations and began bidding.

Our first major wins came from CBP and ICE. Soon after, we secured a contract with TSA, a high-profile agency under intense public and political scrutiny. These contracts, however, could not have been secured without the contract acumen of Sue Ordakowski. Jerry had introduced me to Sue, and in 2002, she became an indispensable part of our team. Her deep understanding of federal procurement and her skill in navigating the complexities of government contracting were essential to our success. While Sue helped us win, execution depended on Toby Luttropp. Toby had worked for a Kroll acquisition in Loveland, Colorado—Kroll Factual Data—and had partnered with me to use that platform as a provider for the TSA contract. We got along so well that I asked him to serve as my deputy and lead the effort to stand up operations in Loveland.

Operating in Colorado, as opposed to Washington, D.C., or

New York, made sense: there was less competition for cleared personnel, and people wanted to stay in Colorado. Toby's steady leadership, operational savvy, and ability to translate policy into practice ensured that our teams on the ground delivered at the level expected from Kroll. After proving ourselves on those initial engagements, we went after the big prize: OPM itself. Winning that contract in 2004 was a defining moment—proof that we could compete in a space thought impenetrable for newcomers.

Our success did not go unnoticed. USIS, which had by then become a private-equity-backed behemoth, accused us of poaching employees and leveraging proprietary knowledge. They sued in Butler, Pennsylvania. We fought back—and prevailed. It was a moment of vindication—not just legally, but strategically. We had taken on the dominant player and not only survived, but thrived. The win underscored a conviction I carried from the courtroom to Kroll: with the right leadership, integrity, and ability to thrive in the regulatory weeds, you can widen the map of what's possible. We were now part of the national security infrastructure. And there would be no turning back.

Chapter 27
The Rescue

While we were methodically building Kroll Government Services into a trusted partner for national security, a storm was battering one of the world's largest financial services firms back in New York.

Eliot Spitzer, my old colleague now serving as Attorney General of New York State, had launched an aggressive investigation into the insurance industry, placing Marsh & McLennan squarely in its sights. The scrutiny threatened not only a major business line, but the firm's credibility, leadership stability, and standing in the market. In that context, MMC—as the company was known—was not looking to expand; it was looking for a lifeline. Its leadership came to believe that lifeline lay in acquiring Kroll. This was not a conventional acquisition, but a strategic deployment of Kroll's credibility to help stabilize a corporate giant under siege. The path from a shared prosecutorial past to a headline-making acquisition was anything but linear.

Eliot Spitzer, Mike Cherkasky, and I had once worked side by side in the Manhattan District Attorney's Rackets Bureau, united by a belief in the power of the law to confront institutional wrongdoing. Years later, that same ethos—refined and elevated to statewide authority—would drive Eliot, as Attorney General, to challenge an industry whose practices he believed had evaded meaningful accountability. The connection was not planned, but the arcs would collide. As Spitzer's investigation unfolded, past and present began to intersect in ways that would leave none of us unchanged. The Rackets Bureau was a tight-knit corps of prosecutors trained under Robert Morgenthau's unrelenting gaze.

It was a demanding place, but also a rare proving ground where young lawyers were entrusted with enormous responsibility and expected to carry it with precision and integrity. That is where I worked alongside Eliot Spitzer, whose presence—even then—

suggested something larger. He was not simply there to learn how to prosecute racketeering cases; he was there to challenge the systemic failures that allowed powerful actors to abuse the public trust.

I remember vividly sitting with Eliot on the day of the 1987 stock market crash—Black Monday. The Dow Jones Industrial Average fell more than 500 points, a staggering 22 percent in a single day. From inside the Rackets Bureau, we watched the markets collapse, shaken by the speed and scale of the decline. I recall lamenting my personal losses—calculated at a few thousand dollars—which, at the time, felt substantial. Eliot, by contrast, was unusually quiet, intensely focused. It would become clear later that he had more at stake, both financially and ideologically. That moment did more than instill a wariness of unchecked financial systems; it reinforced a conviction that public authority could, and should, be used to impose accountability where private restraint had failed.

What none of us could have foreseen was how directly Eliot's eventual ascent to New York State Attorney General would intersect with our professional lives. Absent Spitzer's pressure, the door would not have opened in the way it did. The irony was unmistakable: a prosecution launched by an old friend, under laws designed to reform markets, would ultimately reshape our futures. What follows is the story of how that investigation unfolded—and how it pulled us, however improbably, into its gravitational field.

The Rise of the "Sheriff of Wall Street"

By the time Eliot Spitzer was elected New York State Attorney General in 1998, those of us who had worked with him at the Manhattan DA's Office already knew that he brought a singular intensity to everything he did. He had an eye for systemic wrongdoing, a nose for prosecutorial opportunity, and a prosecutor's instinct to chase the case all the way to the top. Once in office, he wasted little time transforming what had long been viewed as a somewhat sleepy constitutional post into the most feared regulatory force on Wall Street.

Drawing on the expansive powers of the Martin Act—a 1921 statute unique to New York that gave him authority to investigate and bring civil and criminal actions for securities fraud without proving intent—Spitzer set his sights on the financial industry with a force and public visibility that federal regulators seemed either unable or unwilling to match. What made him so effective was not just his use of the law, but his mastery of narrative. He exposed email trails, highlighted conflicts of interest, and gave public voice to practices that had become normalized in boardrooms but appeared outrageous to the average investor or policyholder.

In the wake of the dot-com bust and a series of high-profile accounting scandals—Enron, WorldCom, Tyco—Spitzer stepped into a void of trust in corporate America. His early investigations into research analyst conflicts at Merrill Lynch and other investment banks led to an unprecedented $1.4 billion settlement and forced a structural separation between research and banking functions. From there, he turned to the mutual fund industry, targeting illegal late trading and market timing. At every turn, he articulated a simple theme: the game was rigged, and he was here to set it straight.

His critics accused him of grandstanding and of using the Martin Act's low evidentiary bar to coerce settlements rather than try cases. Eliot seemed to welcome that criticism—if not court it—because it reinforced the persona he had constructed: the outsider with insider knowledge, the prosecutor who had traded courthouse hallways for the bright lights of public accountability. The moniker "Sheriff of Wall Street" wasn't self-styled; it was bestowed by others, and he wore it as a badge of honor.

The Storm at MMC

By the summer of 2004, Marsh & McLennan Companies (MMC) had entered troubled waters. Rumblings of regulatory scrutiny were growing louder, and Eliot Spitzer's increasingly aggressive posture toward the insurance industry made it clear that a reckoning was near. Internally, MMC's leadership understood that the company was vulnerable—not just to reputational damage, but to an existential challenge to its way of doing business.

To the outside world, the acquisition of Kroll may have looked like a bold expansion into corporate intelligence and risk consulting. But inside MMC's executive ranks, the calculation was more urgent and tactical. They weren't just acquiring a firm—they were acquiring a leader. Mike Cherkasky's reputation as a former prosecutor with deep experience navigating complex regulatory terrain made him an asset MMC believed could help them weather the storm ahead. Most importantly, MMC knew that Eliot had once worked for Mike and that the two had a personal relationship. The deal was about Kroll, yes—but it was also clearly about Mike.

When MMC announced the acquisition in mid-2004, Spitzer's investigation was already well underway. Executives understood the move was preemptive—an effort to bring prosecutorial credibility inside before the public reckoning began.

Then the storm broke. Spitzer's civil complaint, filed in October 2004, alleged widespread bid-rigging, kickbacks disguised as contingent commissions, and fraudulent practices that undermined the integrity of the insurance market. MMC, the world's largest broker, stood at the center. Clients fled, shareholders revolted, and public confidence cratered. CEO Jeff Greenberg, who had engineered the Kroll acquisition, was forced out under board pressure.

At that moment, MMC turned to the person it had effectively recruited for this very scenario. Mike Cherkasky was named CEO of MMC. His elevation was swift but logical—it fulfilled the underlying rationale of the acquisition itself.

In hindsight, the deal functioned as a backdoor succession plan. Kroll, absorbed just weeks earlier, suddenly found itself at the heart of MMC's survival strategy. Our mandate expanded overnight. We were no longer just advisors—we embodied MMC's commitment to transparency and reform.

What the Acquisition Changed

Mike took the reins with zeal. He dismantled symbols of excess: the executive dining room closed, company planes sold, chauffeured cars eliminated. Even the in-house shoe-shine service was ended—controversial but intentional, part of redefining the tone at the top.

For a brief period, Mike asked me to serve as his Chief of Staff—a role that proved unsustainable given my responsibilities with the LAPD Monitorship. Still, the shift was unmistakable. We had moved from modest offices on Third Avenue to opulent corporate surroundings. Sitting in my oversized office, I sometimes felt profound dissonance, wondering how a prosecutor who once chased the Westies through Hell's Kitchen had ended up in a space designed to insulate its occupant from reality.

As Mike's responsibilities grew, I assumed greater leadership of the Monitorship. Though our work remained grounded in the same principles, the context had changed entirely. Kroll was no longer just advising institutions—it was reshaping one from within.

The Next Five Years

With Mike steering MMC through crisis, Kroll entered a period of expansion. My own responsibilities multiplied. While continuing to lead the LAPD Monitorship, I grew our federal government business—most notably security-clearance investigations. What began as a targeted response to post-9/11 needs became one of Kroll's largest portfolios. By 2009, we employed more than 1,800 background investigators nationwide.

But federal work was only part of the story. In the years ahead, I would confront wrongful prosecutions, police shootings, bureaucratic resistance, and deeply divided communities. Each assignment represented a new battlefront in the broader mission of justice and integrity.

The acquisition changed our scale and address—but the mission, and the stakes, only grew.

Chapter 28
Detroit

Our success in Los Angeles had firmly established Kroll as a credible and capable institution for managing complex police reform. It also made clear that no two cities, and no two departments, could be approached the same way. So, when the Department of Justice reached out in 2003 to inform us of a new opportunity in Detroit, I was immediately intrigued—but also realistic about the scope and scale. I had no illusions about being able to take on a second monitorship myself, given my other responsibilities, nor did I think it would serve Detroit well.

Detroit was—and still is—a majority-Black city, and its history and culture demanded sensitivity as much as technical skill. Of course, what mattered most was that the monitor possess the integrity, independence, and credibility to earn the community's trust—not that any single demographic box be checked. Representation can support legitimacy, but legitimacy ultimately comes from competence and fairness.

Fortunately, at Kroll we had someone who checked all of the boxes. Sheryl Robinson had recently joined the firm after a distinguished tenure at the Manhattan DA's Office. She was sharp, principled, and an exceptional attorney. Sheryl had both the stature and the steadiness the assignment required. Together, we crafted a response to Detroit's RFP and were invited to interview with the Mayor, Kwame Kilpatrick, the City Attorney, and the Chief of Police. Our approach—frank, rigorous, and rooted in experience—resonated. We were awarded the monitorship.

In the early months, I traveled regularly to Detroit, helping Sheryl establish relationships and assess the department's internal culture and structural challenges. This was Kroll's second major federal monitorship—similar to the Los Angeles monitorship in framework, but far different in tone and environment. Unlike Los

Angeles, Detroit's Consent Decrees (there were two) extended beyond police conduct into the conditions of confinement within the city's holding facilities and jails. These were not marginal concerns—the DOJ's investigation had revealed prolonged detentions under unsanitary and unconstitutional conditions, systemic excessive use of force, and a department that had become functionally untethered from constitutional norms.

The decrees, filed in 2003, addressed wide-ranging failures: deadly force, warrantless witness detention, detainee mistreatment, and illegal arrests. The scale of federal involvement was unprecedented for a city already strained by economic collapse. That collapse was so profound that our very first check from the City actually bounced—a surreal moment that required the federal court to issue a special order ensuring that monitors and consultants would be paid. It was a stark reminder that even reform requires solvency.

The decrees required overhauls of policy and supervision, training, and internal accountability. DPD was instructed to eliminate practices such as detaining witnesses without probable cause and to implement clear tracking mechanisms for use-of-force incidents. The holding cells, some of which had kept individuals for days or weeks in appalling conditions, were subject to court-mandated upgrades in both physical infrastructure and operational protocols.

Implementation was anything but smooth. Detroit was grappling with a fiscal crisis, high turnover in police leadership, and an often-adversarial relationship between City Hall and the Justice Department. The early phase of reform began under Chief Jerry Oliver, appointed by Mayor Kilpatrick in 2002, but his tenure ended abruptly in 2003 after a firearm-transport incident. He was succeeded by Ella Bully-Cummings, a career Detroit officer and the department's first female chief. It was during her tenure that the consent decrees were implemented. Bully-Cummings faced skepticism from some quarters and resistance from others, yet she demonstrated steadiness and resolve under enormous pressure.

After approximately six months of shared leadership of the project, I left active management to Sheryl. Supported by our Kroll team, she persisted in issuing data-driven reports that documented both progress and deficiencies. Her work was grounded in evidence, not politics—an approach that earned credibility with the court even as it drew resistance elsewhere.

Unfortunately, the monitorship was not without its own controversy. Sheryl, by then no longer with Kroll and practicing at a law firm in Baltimore, to which she had taken her role as Monitor, resigned in 2009 following revelations of an inappropriate relationship with Mayor Kilpatrick, who was himself embroiled in legal and ethical scandals that would later lead to his conviction and imprisonment. It was an ignominious end to what had been, for the most part, a powerful example of effective oversight.

The news was deeply disappointing. In retrospect, I do not know whether the relationship began while we worked together in Detroit. I have often asked myself whether I should have seen signs of impropriety earlier—or whether, even if I had, anything could have been done to prevent what followed. These questions linger, and I have no definitive answers. What I do know is that, fortunately for Kroll, Sheryl was no longer with the firm when the allegations became public. Even so, reputational echoes travel far, and for those of us who respected her work, the disappointment was profound.

In a business where your only currency is your reputation for integrity, when you vouch for someone, you are lending them that currency. To watch it be squandered—not by incompetence, but by an alleged lapse in judgment—shook my confidence in my own ability to read people, a skill I had prided myself on since my days interviewing homicide suspects in the precinct.

Despite the cloud that ended her tenure, the work itself endured. The federal court ultimately terminated the decrees in 2016, declaring the Detroit Police Department reformed and compliant with constitutional standards. The scars left by misconduct did not fully heal, nor were all community concerns laid to rest, but

Detroit emerged with a foundation for more just and accountable policing. It remained a lesson— that leadership is not about who is leading, but really about how they are doing it.

Chapter 29
One Step Forward...

The Shooting of Devin Brown

The fatal shooting of thirteen-year-old Devin Brown in February 2005 marked a challenging and defining moment in our tenure as Monitor of the LAPD Consent Decree. At a time when the Department was still working to reestablish trust in communities of color, the incident threatened to undo years of progress in a single morning, thrust the LAPD back into the glare of national attention, and raised profound questions about use-of-force policy, officer training, accountability, and institutional culture.

Brown, an eighth grader, had taken his parents' car without permission and was driving in the early hours of the morning when he ran a red light, triggering a brief police pursuit. The chase ended when the vehicle mounted a sidewalk. Officer Steven Garcia, believing the vehicle was reversing toward him, fired ten rounds—seven of which struck and killed the unarmed teenager. The car, as later determined, was moving at approximately two miles per hour at the time. That single fact—the slow reverse—came to symbolize a chasm between perception and judgment that reform alone could not close.

The community's response was visceral and immediate. Vigils turned to protests, and a sense of betrayal coursed through South Los Angeles. This was more than the death of a child; it was a breach of faith between the LAPD and a community still scarred by decades of mistrust. The tragedy became a catalyst for collective anger—not only about the shooting itself but also about the enduring legacy of systemic inequity and over-policing in Black neighborhoods.

At the same time, the Department's internal investigation became a crucible for evaluating the LAPD's evolving standards under the Consent Decree—particularly the long-contentious policy around shooting at moving vehicles. That policy had been under review before the shooting, but Devin Brown's death forced the issue into the open. Policy-wise, the incident accelerated changes: the LAPD tightened guidelines on both vehicle pursuits and the use of force during vehicle stops, introducing clearer prohibitions against shooting at moving cars except under the most exigent circumstances and expanding de-escalation training for officers. Mayor James Hahn, then facing a difficult re-election campaign, publicly criticized the pace of implementation, underscoring how deeply the shooting had penetrated the city's political and moral consciousness.

The Police Commission found that the use of deadly force violated Department policy. Their ruling became a flashpoint—particularly after an internal Board of Rights, charged with adjudicating violations of policy within the Department, later cleared the officer in a closed-door proceeding shielded by California's Copley Press decision, which significantly curtailed public access to police disciplinary records. The result was a painful contradiction: one body finding the shooting out of policy, another exonerating it—leaving the public with the impression that accountability was optional.

For the monitoring team, this was not an abstract policy debate. It was a stress test of everything the Consent Decree was meant to fix. We were squarely in the middle—navigating community outrage, evaluating the LAPD's investigative response, and determining whether the incident revealed systemic failures. It did. Although the Department's scientific reconstruction was thorough, the shooting exposed deep weaknesses in policy clarity, tactical training, and public communication. It raised the enduring question of whether policy reform can outpace the instincts of culture—or whether culture will always pull policy back toward habit.

Perhaps most telling was the difficulty in reconciling the number of rounds fired with the vehicle's slow movement—even under the stress of an evolving encounter—against the backdrop of a Consent Decree that had, in theory, already begun to change the rules of engagement. That paradox underscored how reform on paper must be reinforced by constant vigilance in practice.

The shooting also reinforced the delicate balance Chief Bratton was attempting to maintain. Bratton understood both the optics and the substance. He invited an FBI review, met with clergy and community leaders, and reaffirmed the Department's commitment to transparency—yet he also stood by the principle of due process for the involved officer. The tension between those dual obligations—community reassurance and internal fairness—became the defining challenge of his leadership. Even when he was right, the optics could make him seem wrong.

The gap between lawful process and public perception is often unbridgeable in moments of tragedy. What mattered, we believed, was that the process be honest, documented, and used to drive institutional learning rather than deflection.

Looking back, the Devin Brown shooting was emblematic of the challenges inherent in institutional reform. Policies can be rewritten; trust must be rebuilt. Policy changes—such as the eventual tightening of restrictions on shooting at moving vehicles—were critical, but they were not sufficient. Culture, perception, and accountability had to evolve in parallel. And while the Consent Decree could mandate procedural safeguards, it could not legislate empathy or discretion. Those had to be learned, practiced, and modeled—over years, not months.

In the end, Devin Brown's death became both a tragedy and a turning point—a grim reminder that reform is never a straight line. It is a continual negotiation between fear and restraint, between authority and humanity, and between what the law allows and what conscience demands.

For a time, many of us in police reform believed that at least one hard-won lesson had finally taken hold. The dangers of shooting at moving vehicles—long recognized by trainers, policymakers, and courts alike—seemed settled. Departments across the country revised their policies, emphasizing disengagement, distance, and repositioning rather than confrontation; officers were taught to get out of the way rather than place themselves, and everyone around them, in mortal danger. The principle was clear: a moving vehicle, absent extraordinary circumstances, should not be met with gunfire. It was one area where policy, training, and experience appeared to have converged.

That sense of closure was profoundly shaken by the January 2026 shooting of Renee Good in Minneapolis during an enforcement operation involving federal immigration agents. Whatever the ultimate findings regarding legality or agency-specific rules of engagement, the incident reopened a debate many believed had been resolved. Once again, an officer confronted a vehicle perceived as a threat; once again, gunfire was chosen over disengagement; and once again, the aftermath raised familiar questions about judgment under stress, tactical alternatives, and the human cost of miscalculation. The episode underscored a sobering reality: reform is neither permanent nor universal. Policy consensus within progressive police departments does not automatically transfer across agencies, missions, or cultures—particularly when federal actors operate under different incentives, training regimes, and accountability structures. The Minneapolis shooting did not negate the lessons of Devin Brown; it reinforced them. It demonstrated how quickly hard-earned clarity can erode, and how vigilance—not confidence—is the true measure of reform.

May Day 2007

But Devin Brown was not the only moment that exposed how fragile the Department's progress remained. Nor was it the last time I would look back on a hard-fought reform and see familiar warnings go unheeded—patterns resurfacing under pressure, even as institutions insisted the lessons had already been learned. Even as policies were rewritten, audits strengthened, and leadership signaled a commitment to cultural change, deep vulnerabilities continued to exist. Within two years, another incident would make that unmistakably clear.

What unfolded on May 1, 2007, in MacArthur Park—during what was supposed to be a peaceful, permitted demonstration—became a stark reminder that reform on paper and reform in practice can diverge sharply, and that the Consent Decree's work was far from complete.

What began as a peaceful May Day rally—a permitted gathering of immigrant-rights advocates—ended with scenes reminiscent of the LAPD's darkest chapters. Officers from Metropolitan Division's B-Platoon advanced on demonstrators and members of the press with batons and less-lethal munitions, dispersing the crowd without a clear or effectively communicated order. The videos that emerged were unmistakable: families running for cover, reporters struck and shoved, and officers firing 146 projectiles into a crowd that, by all accounts, posed no imminent threat.

The internal reviews that followed described a breakdown in command, planning, and basic crowd-control principles. These were not bureaucratic foot faults; they were fundamental failures of judgment, training, and discipline. Dozens of officers faced disciplinary action. A commander was demoted. And the City ultimately paid more than thirteen million dollars to settle claims arising from the violence. It was a blunt reminder that reform on paper is not the same as reform in practice—and that cultural change must be lived consistently, especially in moments of stress.

In the immediate aftermath, I reached out to LAPD leadership to understand how such a collapse could occur after years of structural reform under the Consent Decree. My first call was to Gerry Chaleff, who led the Civil Rights Integrity Division. Gerry picked up the phone, and before I could get two sentences into my inquiry, he cut me off.

"What does this have to do with the Consent Decree?" he asked.

I explained the obvious: that the command-and-control provisions, the Use of Force policies, the training requirements, the deployment protocols—the entire architecture of the Decree—

existed precisely to prevent episodes like MacArthur Park. Gerry pushed back. He insisted the incident had arisen outside the Decree's technical areas of coverage. We went back and forth for several minutes, each argument landing with more irritation than the one before.

At some point, Gerry paused. There was a long silence on the line. And then he said, quietly, "Okay. I see your point."

He did. And so did the Department. MacArthur Park was not merely a public-relations failure or an operational breakdown; it exposed deep vulnerabilities in the Department's ability to internalize reform in real time.

The timing mattered as well. By then, the LAPD Consent Decree had already been extended by the federal judge for an additional three years. The MacArthur Park incident did not cause that extension, but it reinforced its necessity. What had once been anticipated as a five-year process would, in the end, require nine full years of active monitoring of the entire Decree.

In the life of any reform effort, there are moments that test both the system and the people within it. MacArthur Park was one of those moments—a jolt that reminded everyone, including those of us charged with oversight, that progress is never self-executing. Culture can revert. Training can atrophy. Discipline can slip. And the very practices a Decree is meant to eradicate can reappear if vigilance weakens.

As I look back, the incident reinforced a hard truth: police reform is not a straight line, but a continuous negotiation between aspiration and conduct, promise and performance. The May Day melee stood as proof that the work was far from finished—and that the architecture of oversight is only as strong as its daily practice in the Department's most consequential moments. In the immigration enforcement operations in Minneapolis in late 2025 and early 2026, which included the shooting of Renee Good, ICE agents employed crowd-control and use-of-force practices that bore an uncomfortable resemblance to the failures laid bare at MacArthur

Park: weak command structure, inadequate planning, unclear dispersal orders, and an eagerness to escalate force in volatile public settings. What makes the parallel most unsettling is not simply the recurrence of poor tactics, but the institutional asymmetry it exposes. The irony has always been striking to me. At the very moment federal officials and policymakers of DOJ were pressing cities to reform their police departments—to professionalize use of force, strengthen accountability, and internalize restraint—federal law-enforcement agencies were never subjected to comparable scrutiny, oversight, or reform mandates. The result has been a two-tiered system of accountability, one in which hard-won local reforms have been undermined by federal actors operating beyond the reach of the very standards they helped promote. Reform, it turns out, is not only fragile; it is uneven—and that unevenness carries real consequences.

Chapter 30
Cold Cases

The work in Los Angeles was vital, but it was also mostly abstract—battles over policy language, compliance metrics, and political optics. After the heavy lifting of the Consent Decree, I found myself craving the clarity of the old days: a victim, a suspect, and a folder of evidence. I wanted to touch the work again, not just oversee the systems that managed it.

In early 2006, I found myself stepping into a role I hadn't anticipated—serving once again in the trenches of prosecution, this time as a Special Assistant District Attorney in Nassau County. The opportunity arose following the election of Kathleen Rice as District Attorney, a generational shift in a jurisdiction long defined by the formidable yet aging Denis Dillon. Kathleen's campaign emphasized modernization, integrity, and transparency. Helping to drive that message was Meg Reiss, my close colleague and friend at Kroll and a pivotal figure in our LAPD Consent Decree work. Meg's friendship with Kathleen, born during their days in the Brooklyn DA's Office, became the bridge to my eventual involvement.

When Kathleen assumed office, Meg accepted an offer to head the Investigations Division in the newly constituted administration. It wasn't long before she reached out with an intriguing request: Would I be willing to work—pro bono—on a sensitive cold case that had long troubled the office and the community? That case, which occurred less than two miles from the home in which I was raised, was the 1989 murder of 13-year-old Kelly Ann Tinyes in Valley Stream, a case that had led to a conviction years earlier but still raised profound questions about how the original investigation had been handled and whether justice had truly been done.

I happily agreed, and what began as a limited role quickly expanded. Eventually, I was brought into a second reinvestigation—the infamous Friedman case, the subject of the documentary

Capturing the Friedmans. These were not just "cold cases"; they were flashpoints of community memory and institutional accountability. For me, they offered a return to the essence of prosecution—the meticulous, emotionally fraught, pursuit of truth.

Hell on Horton Road

It was one of the most horrifying crimes in the history of suburban Long Island—a case that seemed to shatter the illusion of safety that defined places like Valley Stream. On March 3, 1989, 13-year-old Kelly Ann Tinyes disappeared from her home on a quiet Valley Stream block I had biked along countless times as a boy on my way to Grant Park—a place once ordinary, now unforgettable.

The next day, her mutilated body was discovered under the stairs in the basement of a nearby house belonging to the Golub family. The killer, 21-year-old Robert Golub, was arrested weeks later, convicted in 1990, and sentenced to 25 years to life. It was one of the first U.S. prosecutions to rely on DNA evidence. Yet even after the verdict, a central question lingered: Did Robert act alone?

When Kathleen Rice took office, she pledged to revisit cases that had long been viewed as closed but remained unresolved in the public conscience. The Tinyes case topped that list. At the heart of that persistence was Kelly's father, Richard Tinyes—a man whose grief had hardened into an unwavering demand for truth. He never accepted that Robert Golub had acted without help. His suspicion focused on Robert's younger brother, who was 14 at the time and home that afternoon. Kathleen promised the family that the case would be reexamined.

Meg's request that I serve as Special Assistant DA required no persuasion. To once again pursue a cold homicide, to apply every investigative tool now available, was irresistible. I partnered with Chuck Ribando, a former NYPD sergeant, who was tapped by Kathleen to head her DA Squad. Over several months, we reopened every lead—reviewing the original files, interviewing witnesses, and traveling out of state to chase down the smallest thread of new evidence.

The facts were chillingly familiar. Kelly had received a phone call. Minutes later, she left her house and was last seen entering the Golub home. Inside were the brother and two friends, reportedly smoking marijuana and playing video games. The friends claimed they were unaware of anything else going on in the house—and both passed polygraphs. DNA evidence tied Robert to the murder beyond dispute. But nothing placed the brother in the act itself or indicated that he had conspired to commit the murder.

Still, we had promised the Tinyes family that no stone would go unturned—and we meant it. We retested DNA using modern methods, re-interviewed witnesses, and pursued faint leads that had gone dormant for nearly two decades. Thousands of investigative hours later, the conclusion was clear: suspicion was not proof, and belief was not evidence. There was no legal basis to charge anyone else.

For me, the case became another lesson on the tension between the pursuit of justice and the discipline it demands. Richard Tinyes's firm belief that his daughter's killer had help was unshakable. As a father, I understood that need for resolution; as a prosecutor, I knew that justice could not rest on firm belief alone. The reinvestigation honored Kelly's memory not by producing a new arrest, but by demonstrating that the pursuit of justice still mattered—even when the outcome is at odds with a family's grief and firm belief.

Revisiting the Friedmans

The second case in which I was involved as a Special Nassau County ADA was the reinvestigation of the sexual-abuse prosecution of Jesse Friedman. The case had haunted the county since the 1980s and was revived by Andrew Jarecki's 2003 documentary *Capturing the Friedmans*, which questioned whether Jesse had been wrongfully convicted amid the national hysteria surrounding child-sex-abuse prosecutions of that era.

Both Jesse Friedman and his father, Arnold Friedman, had pleaded guilty—Arnold in 1988, Jesse shortly thereafter—to multiple counts of child molestation arising from computer classes held in their Great Neck home. There was no physical evidence, only testimony from children who had attended the classes. Years later, the Second Circuit Court of Appeals, while denying Jesse's habeas petition on procedural grounds, expressed serious concern about the fairness of the original prosecution. The Court's opinion suggested there was a "reasonable likelihood" that Friedman had been wrongfully convicted and urged "a further inquiry by a responsible prosecutor's office."

District Attorney Kathleen Rice, newly elected and determined to restore confidence in the office, took that admonition seriously. She created a unique review structure: an internal review team of career prosecutors to conduct the factual reinvestigation, and an external Advisory Panel of distinguished experts to oversee the process and assess its integrity. Meg helped design the framework and invited me to join not on the expert team, but as a member of the internal team alongside Assistant District Attorney Madeline Singas, who would later succeed Kathleen as DA and now serves as an Associate Judge on the New York Court of Appeals, New York's highest court. I attended all of the joint meetings with the panel but, in the end, did not actively participate in the drafting of the ultimate DA's report.

The task was narrow in law but broad in scope: to determine whether Jesse Friedman's plea was truly free and voluntary, and whether the evidence still supported his guilt when viewed under modern standards of justice. Over the course of nearly three years, the team examined thousands of pages of case files, reviewed grand jury minutes, evaluated interview transcripts, and re-interviewed witnesses where possible. Claims that suggestive questioning, hypnosis, or the climate of fear in the 1980s had tainted victim testimony were scrutinized. The team also reviewed every statement Jesse himself had made, including those contemporaneous with his plea.

In June 2013, the Nassau County District Attorney's Office

released a 172-page Conviction Integrity Review report. The conclusion was unambiguous: Jesse Friedman was not wrongfully convicted, and his guilty plea was found to have been knowing, intelligent, and voluntary, and the evidence supporting it—though imperfect by modern standards—remained credible.

The external Advisory Panel, which included Barry Scheck, co-founder of the Innocence Project and one of the nation's leading authorities on wrongful convictions, and Mark Pomerantz, then a partner at Paul Weiss and later a senior adviser to the Manhattan District Attorney's Office in its investigation of President Trump, issued a unanimous statement endorsing the Review Team's process and conclusions. The panel wrote that they were "satisfied that the Report represents the considered, good-faith, and careful analysis of experienced prosecutors and investigators," and that "the Review Team's conclusions are reasonable and supported by the evidence it cites."

Within the report itself, there were no formal dissents or minority opinions. The panel emphasized that it had not independently reweighed witness credibility, but that all its members agreed the DA's review had been thorough and professional. Only later, outside the confines of the report, did Barry Scheck publicly urge the release of additional records for further transparency—a call made in the spirit of continued scrutiny rather than disagreement with the findings themselves.

From inside the process, I can attest to the rigor with which every claim was tested. The review was not designed to vindicate the past, but to expose it to light—to ask, honestly, whether an injustice had occurred. After exhaustive inquiry, the answer was no.

For me, the Friedman case echoed the same moral terrain I had walked decades earlier in the Featherstone prosecution and, more recently, in the Tinyes case: the tension between public doubt and institutional duty, between the yearning for closure and the discipline of evidence. It reminded me that re-examination is not always about rewriting history, but often about reaffirming it—

proving, through renewed scrutiny, that the original truth still holds.

Chapter 31
Independent Eyes

During my tenure at Kroll, I was occasionally asked to step outside the traditional boundaries of consent decree monitoring and compliance to conduct fully independent investigations into high-profile and politically sensitive incidents. These assignments often came directly from government entities—civilian oversight bodies, state executives, or police commissions—seeking outside, apolitical expertise in moments of crisis.

Four such matters stand out: two officer-involved shootings in Austin, Texas; an investigation into the hiring and promotion practices of the Tennessee Highway Patrol; and a high-profile San Francisco incident involving senior officers that became known as "Fajitagate." Each presented its own mix of evidentiary gaps, political pressure, and public scrutiny—and together they revealed much about the limits and possibilities of oversight itself.

Tragedy in East Austin

The first Austin case involved the fatal shooting of Kevin Brown by Sergeant Michael Olsen on June 3, 2007. It occurred in the early morning hours at the Elm Ridge Apartments near Chester's Lounge, during "Operation Silent Night," a citywide initiative aimed at reducing violent crime. Olsen and another officer were issuing a noise citation when a private security guard warned that a man might be armed. Moments later, the guard corrected himself, saying the weapon could be with Brown, a Black man in a red shirt.

Without waiting for backup, Olsen approached. Brown appeared startled and ran. Olsen pursued him through a dimly lit courtyard until Brown slowed, partially turned, and—according to Olsen—reached toward his waistband. Olsen stated that he believed Brown was about to draw a gun. Olsen fired four rounds in two volleys: two while Brown was standing and two after he fell. Brown was pronounced dead at the scene. A small-caliber handgun was later found roughly twenty-five feet away along his flight path. Brown was unarmed at the moment he was shot.

The public reaction was immediate and intense. Brown had been shot in the back, and Olsen had a documented history of misconduct. The case quickly became emblematic of Austin's ongoing struggle with race, policing, and trust. The Travis County Grand Jury declined to indict Olsen, but within the department, an internal reckoning followed.

The Internal Affairs Division sustained that Olsen's tactics were reckless—approaching a potentially armed suspect without backup—but ultimately concluded that his use of deadly force was "inconclusive," neither justified nor in violation. That narrow designation stemmed not from the facts themselves but from a report commissioned by the department from Dr. Bill Lewinski of the Force Science Institute. Lewinski's findings, emphasizing officer perception, reaction time, and "threat recognition," created enough doubt to prevent a sustained finding. Without that report, it is likely the administrative charge would have been upheld.

When the City retained my group at Kroll to review the adequacy of the internal investigation, our mandate was not to reinvestigate the shooting but to assess whether the department's process was complete and objective. In our November 27, 2007, report, we concluded that Olsen's tactics were deeply flawed and that his decision to pursue alone likely precipitated the fatal encounter. Yet, because of missing evidence—no video, no eyewitnesses to the moment of the shooting, and the existence of the Lewinski Report—we could not say the "inconclusive" finding was unsupportable.

While Austin PD appeared to rely on the Lewinski Report's conclusions as authoritative, we treated it with skepticism. We recognized, even then, that the "science" in the report was open to question. Years later, researchers have sharply criticized Force Science's methods, calling for transparent data, replicable results, and genuine scientific rigor before such theories are used to justify deadly force.

That debate remains relevant to me today. Under the Aurora Consent Decree, we have insisted that any claim to "science"—particularly in use-of-force training or review—must withstand the scrutiny of empirical validation. The Kevin Brown case taught an early version of that lesson: unproven science, accepted uncritically, can have real-world consequences for justice and accountability.

The Shooting of Nathaniel Sanders

Two years later, on May 11, 2009, another tragedy unfolded in Austin. Officer Leonardo Quintana fatally shot nineteen-year-old Nathaniel Sanders II and seriously wounded Sir Valience Smith during a confrontation at the Walnut Creek Apartments. Acting on information that a distinctive vehicle had been linked to recent robberies, Quintana detained the driver without backup or activating his mobile video recorder. When support arrived, it was determined that two other young men were asleep inside the car. Without a tactical plan or clear coordination, Quintana approached Sanders, who was in the back seat, alone, spotted a gun in Sanders' waistband, and attempted to seize it. A struggle followed. Quintana retreated and fired four rounds through the rear window, killing Sanders and wounding Smith.

Our external review, again commissioned by the City, found that Quintana's tactics were unsound, his decision-making poor, and the Internal Affairs investigation was tainted by bias, reflected in the language contained in several internal IA emails. The absence of video evidence only deepened public skepticism. When we released our report in September 2009, it reignited community anger and exposed systemic deficiencies in Austin PD's approach to internal accountability.

At the time, Chief Art Acevedo publicly disagreed with our findings—not just in the Sanders case but also in the earlier Kevin Brown review. For years thereafter, Art viewed me with distrust, perhaps seeing our reports as attacks on the department rather than calls for reform. From a distance, he maintained his misgivings.

Years later, when Art served as Interim Chief in Aurora,

Colorado, our paths collided. We agreed to disagree about the past—but also discovered shared ground in the present. What began as professional tension evolved into genuine collaboration. Art became a partner in reform and, ultimately, a friend. Time, perspective, and purpose had replaced tension with mutual respect.

The Tennessee Highway Patrol

In late 2005, Governor Phil Bredesen of Tennessee found himself confronting a crisis. The Tennessee Highway Patrol was engulfed in scandal following a series of exposés in The Tennessean revealing political patronage, unethical hiring, and the sale of honorary ranks to donors and insiders. Promotions appeared to follow campaign contributions more than merit.

The governor suspended promotions and brought in my Kroll group to conduct an independent investigation. I led a team that included Tom Frazier, David B. Mitchell, and Sheldon Greenberg. Over several weeks, we reviewed thousands of documents, visited field offices across the state, and interviewed dozens of troopers, district attorneys, and political officials.

Our findings revealed significant systemic failures. Political favoritism was not an occasional abuse—it was the operating system. Hiring lists were manipulated; residency rules falsified; background checks ignored. Internal Affairs was decentralized to the point of paralysis. In some cases, troopers with red-flag histories had been hired or promoted with little oversight.

Our March 2006 report proposed sweeping reforms: a merit-based billeting system for hiring, statewide promotion transparency, mandatory polygraph and credit checks, and centralization of Internal Affairs functions. The most ambitious recommendation called for the creation of a Department of Law Enforcement—a merger of the Highway Patrol and the Tennessee Bureau of Investigation—intended to professionalize the system and insulate it from political pressure.

Governor Bredesen embraced the findings and began

implementing reforms, though not the merger recommendation. Culture began to shift. The investigation became a model for how independent fact-finding can enhance public trust while reinforcing the legitimacy of those in power.

What struck me most was not the scale of the misconduct, but how quietly it had been tolerated. The corruption had crept upward from years of complacency at the top. Ultimately, reform depended not on the exposure of wrongdoing, but on the will to fix it.

Fajitagate

In 2004, the City of San Francisco quietly retained my Kroll group to review the Police Department's handling of a bizarre but consequential incident—one that began as a drunken street brawl and became a catalyst for leadership upheaval. Three off-duty officers, including the son of an assistant chief, allegedly assaulted two men over a bag of steak fajitas. The episode, soon dubbed "Fajitagate," would shake the department to its core.

The assignment was not to re-investigate the assault, but to evaluate SFPD's Internal Affairs process: how the department investigated itself and how the chain of command responded once the case became public. The findings were delivered confidentially to Chief Heather Fong and the Police Commission. The report, though never released, was blunt about cultural blind spots, procedural weaknesses, and the need for clear investigative guardrails.

The fallout from the incident was seismic. Chief Earl Sanders and Assistant Chief Alex Fagan Sr. of the SFPD were indicted in the "Fajitagate" scandal for alleged obstruction of justice in the investigation of off-duty officers—though the case ultimately collapsed and the charges were dismissed. Both men left the force.

In the aftermath of the scandal, two figures emerged whose careers would later carry national significance. Kamala Harris defeated the incumbent San Francisco District Attorney in 2003, offering voters a professional and reform-minded alternative at a moment when the office's credibility had been shaken; she would later go on to serve as California Attorney General and Vice President of the United States. George Gascón, whom I knew from his years at the LAPD under Bill Bratton, was appointed San Francisco Police Chief in 2009 as the City continued to grapple with unresolved failures of discipline and accountability, and in 2011 he succeeded Harris as District Attorney.

It was a remarkable chain reaction set in motion by an absurd event. A fight over fajitas had upended a city's police leadership and played a part in launching the careers of two future national figures. For me, the assignment reinforced a lesson I had seen repeatedly (and which has become a standard article of faith): the cover-up is often greater than the crime.

The Thread That Connects

Taken together, these four cases—each distinct in geography, scope, and institutional culture—illustrated the breadth of challenges we confronted at Kroll and the different ways in which integrity, accountability, and reform could be tested. In Austin, we were confronted with the limits of internal review and the human cost of flawed tactics; in Tennessee, we showed how political patronage can hollow out an institution from within; and in San Francisco, we confronted the cultural inertia that can turn a minor incident into a crisis of legitimacy. Each assignment required a different balance of rigor and restraint, empathy and candor. Collectively, they defined the work we were doing during that period—quietly, methodically, and without fear or favor—grounded in the belief that the pursuit of truth, however uncomfortable, is the most enduring form of reform.

That, in the end, is what independent investigation must mean. It is not about rewriting history. It is about illuminating it—quietly, methodically, and truthfully—so that institutions can find their way back to the integrity they were meant to embody.

Chapter 32
The Campaign

Return and Reunion

As my work at Kroll continued, a familiar face re-entered my sphere in what would prove much more consequential than I could then imagine.

In 2004, after sixteen years in Seattle, Cy Vance, my comrade from the Rackets Bureau, returned to New York City with his wife, Peg, and their two children, Clare and Simon. His decision to come back home followed a highly successful run in private practice, where he had built a reputation as a formidable trial attorney and advocate for civil rights and corporate accountability. Though he had long carried both the benefits and the burden of a prominent name—his father, Cyrus Vance Sr., had served as Secretary of State under President Jimmy Carter—Cy had indisputably stepped out of that shadow. His legal work in Seattle included securing a landmark $72.5 million gender discrimination settlement against Boeing, defending high-profile clients, and establishing himself as a principled and measured figure in the courtroom.

Shortly after his return, we reconnected. We had grown close during our years in the Rackets Bureau of the Manhattan DA's Office, but with Cy's relocation to the West Coast and my own shift to a career in risk management and oversight, our friendship had lapsed into infrequent contact. His return reignited that bond quickly and naturally. We fell back into a familiar rhythm of conversation and collaboration, and almost immediately began speaking about the possibility of his running for District Attorney in 2009. The idea was, at that stage, speculative—Bob Morgenthau was still in office and showed no clear signs of retiring, despite being in his late eighties. But Cy was serious. We both recognized the rare opportunity that lay ahead: a chance to renew and modernize the institution we had come up in, and to build a campaign that could carry that legacy forward.

Building the Campaign

As the time for decisions grew closer, the thought of another four-year term for Morgenthau, one taking him to the age of ninety-four, naturally fueled speculation that a transition might be on the horizon. Cy had spoken to Morgenthau about his desire to succeed him, but Morgenthau remained uncommitted, although he did not foreclose the possibility. As such, it was clear we needed to be prepared. It was decided to lay the necessary groundwork. Cy began running, not as a challenger, but as a successor. The campaign would never be about unseating Morgenthau, but rather about being prepared to carry the office forward should Morgenthau decide to retire.

We began meeting regularly, discussing vision, messaging, and campaign infrastructure. I assumed the role of Campaign Treasurer and senior advisor. Mike Cherkasky, whose campaign I had managed twelve years earlier, was likewise supportive, though his attention was divided by the demands of steering Marsh & McLennan through its corporate storm. Peg was the driving force—brilliant, determined, and unshakably convinced that Cy had both the temperament and the vision to lead.

Complicating the early calculus was our understanding that Morgenthau had privately conveyed to Dan Castleman—then serving as Chief of the Investigations Division and a former colleague from our Rackets Bureau days—that he would support him should he choose not to seek re-election. Dan was both a professional peer and a friend, which made the situation particularly delicate. As the campaign field began to take shape, the complexity deepened. Although Dan never entered the race, two additional candidates did, each of whom I knew personally. One was Rich Aborn, a respected public safety advocate and former colleague in the Office with whom I had a close and collegial relationship. The other was Leslie Crocker Snyder, more of a professional acquaintance, a former judge and alumna of the Office who had served under Frank Hogan and during the early years of the Morgenthau administration.

On February 27, 2009, Morgenthau publicly announced that he would not seek re-election. Cy announced his candidacy ten days later on March 9. The race was on.

Fundraising began immediately. Our message was disciplined: Cy would honor the legacy of the Office while modernizing its approach to justice. With multiple strong contenders, our task was to present Cy as the candidate of experience, moderation, and integrity—a bridge between eras, not a break from them.

Navigating the Field

From the very beginning, our campaign was animated by the principle that we were running to continue and build upon the extraordinary legacy Morgenthau had created over more than three decades as District Attorney. That message shaped the tone, structure, and strategy of the campaign itself. Cy had served with distinction in the Office under Morgenthau during the 1980s, and despite his time away in Seattle, had remained deeply committed to the values of public service and prosecutorial discretion that Morgenthau championed. Our objective was clear: demonstrate that Cy was the candidate most capable of carrying that tradition forward while bringing new ideas suited to a changing world.

Even in those early days of planning, it was clear that Cy would not be running in a vacuum—each opponent brought a distinct identity, rhetorical posture, and policy emphasis to the contest.

Aborn cast himself as the bold "progressive prosecutor," stressing prevention and reform over retrenchment: he proposed a "PreventStat" data-driven tracking system, sought greater collaboration with defense counsel to channel nonviolent offenders into treatment rather than incarceration, pledged to prosecute gun trafficking aggressively and to modernize lineups and interrogation processes (including videotaping) to guard against wrongful convictions. He won the endorsement of the Working Families Party and labeled himself the candidate willing to break from "business as usual" in the Morgenthau era.

In contrast, Leslie Crocker Snyder leaned heavily on her reputation as a tough, no-nonsense former prosecutor and judge. Though initially less specific on reformist technicalities, she criticized the DA's office for having grown "stale and reactive," promised to bring vehicular homicide and negligent homicide cases before grand juries more routinely, and pledged to meet personally with families of victims even when charging decisions were constrained by statute. She also had the personal brand of "the judge's candidate," signaling a continuity of prosecutorial toughness.

Meanwhile, Cy sought a middle path between these poles. His platform emphasized community-based justice—allocating prosecutors who would be assigned to precincts and neighborhoods, deploying resources in a way that aligned with local conditions, and balancing enforcement with discretion. He pledged that white-collar crime and street crime would be treated with equivalent seriousness and promised the formation of a Conviction Integrity Panel to review past cases where questions of actual innocence had been raised.

In effect, Aborn sought to reimagine prosecutorial paradigms; Snyder to restore prosecutorial assertiveness; and Cy to modernize and humanize the legacy of Morgenthau while keeping his feet firmly on both the law-and-order and reform tracks.

At its base, our campaign remained focused on demonstrating Cy's deep qualifications, progressive vision, and moral authority to lead the Office into its next chapter. But we always knew that in a crowded and competitive field, with multiple strong contenders and overlapping circles of professional loyalty, a single endorsement had the potential to change the race.

That endorsement came—crucially—on August 19, 2009, less than a month before the Democratic primary, and was due, at least in part, to Peg's relationship with Morgenthau's wife, Lucinda Franks Morgenthau. Robert M. Morgenthau, the Boss and a towering figure in New York's legal world, publicly declared that Cyrus R. Vance Jr. was the "best qualified" candidate to succeed him. In doing so, he highlighted Cy's prosecutorial service under his leadership and his substantial legal accomplishments in the years since. The New York Times reported on the endorsement, noting its symbolic and strategic importance in a city where Morgenthau's word still carried tremendous weight. And an endorsement from the New York Times followed closely.

Those endorsements redefined the trajectory of the campaign. It solidified the narrative of continuity and competence that we had worked so hard to build, and it helped unify many of Morgenthau's supporters behind Cy. It also provided voters with an implicit contrast: of all the candidates in the field, only one had earned the explicit confidence of the legendary District Attorney. That moment—Morgenthau handpicking Cy, lending his voice and reputation—was not just a political boost; it was an emotional vindication of the path we had chosen and the manner in which we had pursued it.

Etan Patz

The campaign was personal, politically complex, and increasingly high profile. With the endorsement of Morgenthau and the Times, Cy was the frontrunner, but not necessarily a shoe-in.

I continued in multiple roles during the campaign, serving as Treasurer, senior advisor, and, on occasion, surrogate. I also helped develop policy positions and talking points, ensuring that Cy's platform spoke to public safety and justice in equal measure. One of the most consequential contributions I made came in the form of a suggestion—a nudge, really—that ultimately shaped one of the most high-profile cases of Cy's tenure and demonstrated his willingness to confront the unresolved legacies of the Office he was poised to inherit.

Etan vanished on May 25, 1979, during my first year in the Office. A six-year-old boy on his way to the school bus in SoHo had his face among the first ever featured on a milk carton. Despite decades of effort, no one had ever been held accountable. The case had grown cold, and the public had all but resigned itself to the idea that it would remain unsolved. During the campaign, I encouraged Cy to meet with Etan's father, Stan Patz—a man who had never given up hope and who continued to advocate for justice on his son's behalf. That meeting was not arranged for political optics; it was born of a belief that a new District Attorney ought to listen to the victims of the past as well as to the needs of the present.

Stan Patz had publicly endorsed Leslie Crocker Snyder. He had long viewed her as the candidate most committed to convening a grand jury on Etan's disappearance and said he felt "beholden" to her for taking up his cause when he believed the Office had turned him away. Snyder's pledge drew headlines—and some criticism for prejudging a prosecutorial step—but it also explained Patz's stance. Our path with Etan's father remained different by design: to listen first, then reopen the case on the merits—an approach Cy ultimately carried into office.

The meeting, which I attended, was emotional and sobering. But it also became catalytic. It led Cy, after his election, to order a full reexamination of the case. That decision ultimately resulted in the indictment and conviction of Pedro Hernandez, a former bodega clerk who confessed to luring Etan into a basement and killing him. The verdict seemed to bring long-sought closure to a family that had waited thirty-three years.

It's not often that a campaign decision becomes the basis for a landmark prosecution, but the Etan Patz case was exactly that. For Cy, it underscored the importance of listening. For me, it affirmed what I had always believed about Cy—he had the judgment and moral clarity to lead the Office with both compassion and resolve.

Yet, in a cruel twist, in July 2025, the conviction of Pedro Hernandez—after having been affirmed through all state appeals—was overturned by the federal Court of Appeals, which found that errors in the jury instructions regarding his confessions required that he either be retried or released. It was a stark reminder that even cases pursued with care and conviction can remain unsettled decades later. What had long been seen as unbearably delayed closure for the Patz family became even more unbearable, with the prospect of justice delayed yet again. As of this writing, the case stands at a painful crossroads: Hernandez's conviction has been vacated, prosecutors have indicated they may seek further review in the Supreme Court, and Etan's family faces the possibility of yet another trial in a story that has haunted New York for generations.

Cy won the Democratic primary on September 15, 2009, with 44 percent of the vote, besting Snyder and Aborn in a closely watched contest. In Manhattan, where the Democratic primary all but determines the general election outcome, that victory effectively sealed the result. The general election in November, indeed, turned out to be merely a formality; Cy took over 90 percent of the vote and was sworn in as District Attorney on January 1, 2010.

The swearing-in took place in the Office of the County Clerk in an understated ceremony. I hosted a luncheon for family and key members of the campaign team that day at Forlini's, the iconic restaurant and watering hole, which in my early days in the Office served as after-work central for decompression. I had not been back in years but was greeted by the owners as an old friend helping to usher in a new era.

After the election, Cy asked me to join him in the Office. It was an honor to be asked, but the timing was not right. I was heading the new KeyPoint Government Solutions, the spin-off of my government services business from Kroll, which required my full attention. I told Cy that the door wasn't closed—only that the moment wasn't quite yet. Five years later, the opportunity would arise again under far different circumstances.

Chapter 33
Crossroads

Mike's appointment as CEO marked the start of a turbulent realignment inside MMC. The crisis that had forced Jeff Greenberg's departure now demanded not only reputational repair but also cultural reinvention. From the first days of his tenure, Mike drew heavily on the Kroll ethos—transparency, investigation, and control—to steady a corporation unaccustomed to public scrutiny. For those of us who had come from Kroll, it was clear that our methods were now being tested on a much larger stage.

Mike steadied the ship. He settled with the Attorney General, slowed the client exodus, and restored a measure of calm.

I watched these developments closely. At the time, I was running Kroll Government Services (KGS), which encompassed not only the LAPD monitorship but also our growing federal security clearance investigation business. That line of work was beginning to expand rapidly, and while Mike had encouraged me to pursue it, his enthusiasm became more guarded when it came to what could potentially become our largest customer: the Office of Personnel Management (OPM)—the agency that not only oversaw all federal security clearances but was also the single largest direct client for clearance investigations.

I remember vividly an introductory meeting in late 2003 at OPM's Iron Mountain facility, from which they supervised security clearance operations. Along for the trip was Mike Shmerling, who headed Kroll Background America. Sitting at the table, I worried that Mike might decide to entrust Shmerling, rather than me, with leading the pursuit of OPM's business. My concern was only heightened when, in that meeting, Cherkasky unexpectedly voiced aloud his doubts about whether Kroll even wanted the contract—remarks I found so ill-timed that I still recall giving him a discreet kick under the table. Whether his comments reflected genuine uncertainty or simply an offhand remark, I never knew. In the end, however, Mike chose to have me continue leading the effort, for which I remain ever grateful. In 2004, we won the OPM contract—our entry into the largest, most exacting market in the space.

By 2007, MMC's emergency had passed, yet its stock was lagging peers. The diversified structure—Marsh, Mercer, Kroll, Guy Carpenter, Oliver Wyman, and Putnam—was increasingly framed as a drag rather than a strength by analysts and industry observers. Shareholder impatience mounted.

I also sensed that MMC's appetite for government business was waning. It wasn't their world. The culture of long-cycle, compliance-heavy government contracts did not mesh with the fast-moving, revenue-driven ethos of a global insurance and consulting conglomerate. Even Kroll's unique value proposition was being diluted by attempts to cross-sell its services into MMC's broader ecosystem. When Mike announced the sale of Putnam Investments in 2007, it was clear to those watching that the divestiture of non-core assets had become the strategy. That did not bode well for my unit of Kroll—or, for that matter, Kroll itself.

Then came the announcement that truly altered the playing field. In December 2007, MMC and its board announced that Mike would be stepping down as CEO. According to public reporting at the time, the decision was driven by poor financial performance, a 19 percent drop in stock price, and increasing investor agitation. The board, led by Chairman Stephen Hardis, concluded it was time for a leadership change. For me, however, the more seismic news came shortly thereafter: Mike would be taking the helm of USIS—our chief competitor in the federal investigations market.

To say I was stunned would be an understatement. USIS's dominant position and its growing backlog were what opened the door for KGS in the first place, and Mike had been a strategic partner in our shared belief that USIS needed to be challenged—for market reasons, but also because the public interest demanded consistent, high-quality, and timely work. And now, he was going to lead them.

I knew that we shared a belief that the way federal security clearance investigations were conducted was problematic, and I had clearly hoped that together we might be able to help reform the methodology. At the time, though, I was less concerned about Mike's new role than I was about the future of KGS at MMC. While there was no immediate impact, I understood that my position within MMC—never fully understood or appreciated by corporate leadership other than Mike—was tenuous, at best. KGS was not part of the company's future, and with Mike gone, there were fewer, if any, internal advocates who understood the value of what we had built. The writing was on the wall.

It was a cold realization. In the DA's Office, you knew that no matter how bad the case got, your partner had your back. In the corporate world, I was learning, alliances dissolve the moment the org chart shifts. I was no longer part of a team saving a company; I was an exposed asset in a portfolio that no longer made sense to its owners.

Still, during the remainder of Mike's tenure at MMC and through his leadership at USIS, we kept in close communication. We were still best of friends. We talked about the failings of the background investigations industry, the lack of innovation, and the importance of integrity in a field too often driven by metrics over meaning. But those conversations took on a slightly different tone, given that we were, in the purest sense, competitors.

The next chapter in my professional journey would be shaped by the steps I would need to take to ensure that KGS remained not only viable but also became the premier provider of government clearance investigations. The moment to separate from MMC was approaching, and with it, the need to chart a new path—independent of both Mike and MMC.

Chapter 34

Betting on Independence

With Mike's departure and MMC's strategic focus turning increasingly away from government services, it became clear that Kroll Government Services would need to chart a new future. A classic management presentation book was prepared, and we launched a road show—a series of meetings between our leadership team and prospective buyers. These sessions provided a detailed view of our operations and the unit's potential as a standalone company.

There was no shortage of interest. Four serious bidders emerged: two strategic buyers with complementary businesses and two private equity firms. In the end, the best fit—by far—was Veritas Capital, a firm with deep expertise in government-facing sectors, including national security, intelligence, and critical infrastructure. Veritas understood our world. They knew that success in the government space depended as much on credibility and precision as on scale.

Veritas had built a formidable reputation for deep domain expertise and hands-on support of its portfolio companies. At the time, the firm was led by Bob McKeon, its founder and visionary leader. Tragically, McKeon died in 2012, a loss felt deeply across Veritas. Following his passing, Ramzi Musallam, a longtime partner and my initial primary contact at Veritas, took over as CEO. Under his leadership, Veritas would become one of the most successful firms in the industry, and Ramzi himself would go on to be counted among the wealthiest individuals in America.

The deal with Veritas was consummated in 2009. I was now the president and CEO of a portfolio company of one of the most respected private equity firms in the world. For the next five years, I worked most directly with Joe Benevides, a junior partner at the time. Joe was thoughtful, responsive, and focused—an ideal counterpart. Compared to my experience with MMC and Mike's reflections on Providence, the private equity firm he was working with at USIS, my relationship with Veritas stood out as especially positive. They were supportive in all the right ways: engaged when needed, but never meddlesome. They allowed me to run the business as I saw fit. Of course, it helped that we were doing quite well. I've always wondered how that relationship might have looked had we struggled. But in our case, success enabled autonomy.

Personally, I chose to bet on myself and my team. I rolled all of my payout from Kroll into the new entity. Combined with equity grants that vested over five years, I had a significant ownership stake in the company. On paper, this looked like a standard executive maneuver, but in reality, it was a moment of terrifying clarity. I was pushing my chips to the center of the table—betting the security I had built for T and the kids on my ability to outmaneuver a dominant competitor in a volatile market. I remember signing the documents with a steady hand while my stomach churned, knowing that if I was wrong, there was no safety net this time. It was not just a financial decision; it was a statement of belief in our mission and my friends and colleagues who had built KGS from the ground up.

We needed a new name. We wanted to maintain continuity with the KGS acronym, and ultimately landed on KeyPoint Government Solutions. The logo we created featured a five-pointed star, with one point shaded blue to stand out from the four gray points—our "key point." It represented our focus, our clarity of mission, and our differentiation in the marketplace.

Our headquarters remained distributed: I was based in New York, where I worked closely with my highly capable assistant, Victor Cabrera. We initially operated out of the Chrysler Building, with a terrace that stood eye-level with its famed gargoyles, before relocating to offices on West 52nd Street. Operational leadership and field administration were centered in Fairfax, Virginia. This was where Sue Ordakowski and Dave Kervin spent most of their time, courting new business and dealing administratively with the business we had. Loveland, Colorado continued to be our main base of operations, a move that, because of the need for security clearances for our people, made a great deal of sense. There was not the same competition for those with clearances as there was in the DC metro area, and everyone loved living in Colorado. Once you came, you stayed. Lastly, we had set up review and IT operations in Butler, Pennsylvania, strategically situated near Iron Mountain and OPM's own administrative headquarters.

Long before the days of ubiquitous video conferencing, I insisted that we hold daily meetings via video conferencing. Before Zoom there was Polycom, which for a period owned the video conferencing market. The equipment was expensive, but I knew that it was the best way to deal with the multiple locations that were required for our operations.

At the time of the spinout, KeyPoint employed approximately 1,800 investigators operating nationwide, nearly all of whom worked remotely. These investigators covered every town and village across the country, conducting interviews of those seeking clearance, as well as their friends, families, employers, neighbors, and landlords. Over the next five years, our investigator ranks would double. What we had built was not merely a business unit—it was a national enterprise dedicated to supporting national security through thorough, professional investigations. And now, it stood on its own.

The spinout was more than a transaction—it was a rebirth. We were no longer a subsidiary within a sprawling global enterprise; we were fully independent, masters of our own trajectory.

With the help of Toby Luttropp, Sue Ordakowski, Carolyn Symsack, Gary Coombs, Dan Sweet, and hundreds of others who carried the work forward, the next several years became a period of relentless growth, innovation, and adaptation. We built systems, refined methodologies, expanded training, and scaled operations without losing the values that had made us successful.

These years would come to define the culture of KeyPoint

Government Solutions—disciplined, mission-driven, and quietly ambitious. What began as a spinout born of necessity evolved into something far greater: a company built on integrity, sustained by purpose, and strengthened by the belief that doing essential work well is its own reward.

Chapter 35
The Surge

The period following the 2009 spinout of KeyPoint Government Solutions was one of the most ambitious and energizing stretches of my professional life. We had independence, backing from Veritas Capital, and, most importantly, control. No parent company telling us to stay in our lane. No one diluting the mission. For the next five years, we scaled aggressively, modernized relentlessly, and—without quite saying it out loud—set out to reshape a federal background investigation industry that had grown complacent.

By then, the LAPD monitorship had reached its natural end. That work had consumed nearly a decade of my life. We had come into a department many believed was structurally incapable of reform and left it measurably different. A Harvard Kennedy School study found that public satisfaction with the LAPD rose from about 22 percent in the early days of the Decree to more than 80 percent by the time we exited—a radical swing in confidence and legitimacy, particularly in communities that had every historical reason to distrust the police. That, for me, mattered. But Los Angeles was, at last, on its own two feet, and the center of gravity shifted fully to KeyPoint.

The earlier legal battles with USIS had already played out during my final years at Kroll, but the competitive landscape they shaped remained. By 2010, KeyPoint was preparing to take them on directly. USIS was still the dominant force in the federal background investigation space, and we were methodically positioning ourselves to challenge that dominance.

From the start, my goal at KeyPoint wasn't just to compete with the large federal contractors in the personnel security space—USIS, CACI, and MSM. It was to surpass them.

The work itself was simple to describe and maddening to

execute: we were responsible for conducting the background investigations used to grant or deny security clearances across the federal government. These investigations determine who gets access to classified information, who could sit behind an NSA console, and who had a badge at a nuclear facility. It wasn't glamorous, but it was foundational to national security. Do it well, and no one will know your name. Do it badly, and the consequences are on the front page.

We had a clear strategy: grow through operational excellence, not shortcuts.

At that moment, the Office of Personnel Management (OPM) controlled nearly every aspect of how clearance investigations were to be performed. The prescribed model was rigid, and, in my view, outdated, inefficient to the point of dysfunction. Investigators were required to chase down childhood acquaintances, former landlords, and long-ago supervisors in person, sometimes across multiple states, regardless of whether those sources had meaningful insight into the subject's suitability. Internet research—obvious, basic, responsible due diligence—was essentially off-limits. Logical follow-up leads were discouraged if they did not fit within predefined boxes. The system valued process compliance over investigative sense.

In other words, it felt as though the system had been built for paperwork, not for discovering substantive truth.

We couldn't change the federal rules, but we could build a company that operated inside those rules with more discipline, more precision, and more intelligence than anyone else.

So, we engineered the business.

The talent we had brought in during the early days understood the space and was not afraid to rethink old workflows. Two of my most important hires were Jon Elliott and Dave Reiber, data specialists who became architects of one of our most important advantages: our internal case distribution and routing engine.

The logic was straightforward. We were paid by the case. Every hour of investigator time that was wasted—on travel, on inefficiency, on administrative friction—was money burned. We built a routing system that assigned investigations based on geography, caseload, and investigator capacity, to cut dead time between interviews. Field investigators could complete more interviews per day, in a tighter radius, with fewer wasted miles. That wasn't just cost control. That was throughput and consistency at scale.

And critically, we did it while continuously improving quality. From the outset, I pushed the idea that KeyPoint's competitive edge would not come from cutting corners but from absolute integrity in execution. Our review protocols were tight. Our internal quality controls were aggressive. Training emphasized clarity, accuracy, and documentation. If we made a representation to the federal government, it had to be true. That philosophy would turn out to be one of the most important differentiators in our industry when the reckoning came.

Because while we were building, USIS was confronting mounting operational and reputational problems.

The Collapse of USIS

USIS was, for years, the dominant name in federal background investigations. They had inherited the government's own investigative arm when OPM privatized it in the 1990s. That head start translated into market dominance. Over time, that dominance appeared to breed complacency.

In 2011, the first crack went public. A whistleblower named Blake Percival filed a False Claims Act suit alleging that USIS had been "flushing" cases—in effect, certifying background investigations as complete and submitting them to OPM for payment even when crucial steps had not actually been performed. As later described by the Department of Justice in its filings and public statements, hundreds of thousands of files—more than 665,000, roughly 40 percent of total production—had allegedly been pushed through without the required quality review.

I want to be clear about one thing. The decisions that led to those practices predated Mike Cherkasky's arrival in the USIS orbit, and I am convinced they were kept from him by USIS leadership. Mike did not build that culture and would not have tolerated it had he known.

The damage to USIS was catastrophic. And it got worse.

In 2013, two names changed the conversation in Washington: Edward Snowden and Aaron Alexis. Snowden, a former NSA contractor, leaked a vast trove of classified surveillance documents, triggering an international firestorm. Alexis, a Navy contractor, shot and killed twelve people at the Washington Navy Yard. When news like that breaks, the world sees a tragedy, but if you run a security clearance investigations company, you feel a distinct, sickening drop in your gut. You immediately scramble to check the logs: Did we clear him? Was it one of ours? Even if you trust your process, the possibility that a file carrying your company's stamp might be linked to a mass shooting or a national betrayal was a haunting, physical weight that never quite left you. As it turned out, both had cleared federal background checks that, according to press reports and subsequent government statements, had been processed by USIS.

To be perfectly honest, I do not believe that any contractor—including KeyPoint—could have "caught" either man under the investigative rules that existed at the time. The protocols were too mechanical, too constrained, and in some ways almost willfully blind to emerging risk factors like online behavior, sudden grievance escalation, or psychological volatility. But logic and context don't matter much once a story hits the front page. The narrative hardened quickly: the system was broken, and USIS was the face of that failure.

By then, Providence Equity Partners (which had folded USIS into a holding company called Altegrity and later added Kroll and a private sector background screening company called HireRight, in an effort to build a full-spectrum risk and investigations conglomerate) began reshuffling leadership. Mike left at the end of 2011 and was replaced by Sharon Rowlands, an executive known for driving profitability.

I liked Sharon personally. We met several times after she took over. But unlike with Mike, I had no instinct to hold back. I made it known that KeyPoint was in the market for strong mid-level managers—people who knew the work, understood the stakes, and maybe wanted out of an environment that increasingly looked unsteady. We hired some of the best people USIS had.

In 2014, shortly after I left for my position of Chief of Staff at DANY, a cyberattack—widely reported as being linked to Chinese state actors—breached USIS systems and compromised the personal information of more than 25,000 federal employees with access to sensitive material. KeyPoint also experienced a cyber intrusion that drew intense scrutiny. But for reasons that are still not clear to me, OPM treated the breach at USIS as the final nail in the coffin and terminated their contracts. The work that USIS was performing was shifted to the other providers, including KeyPoint, which got the bulk of the work and became the leading primary contractor for federal security clearances. The largest player in the field—the company that had once seemed untouchable—was effectively gone.

As a result of getting this work, KeyPoint's investigative workforce, which by 2014 had doubled to more than 3,000 investigators nationwide, burgeoned to more than 5,000. The moment was defining. KeyPoint had moved from challenger to standard-bearer.

And yet, even at our strongest, I understood how fragile that position was. One ethical failure can end you. One system failure can end you. Our credibility was our currency.

A Return to Public Integrity

Even as KeyPoint expanded, I occasionally returned to my

roots when asked to handle matters touching on public integrity. In 2010, at the request of Mike Cherkasky—then also serving as the pro bono chair of the New York State Commission on Public Integrity—I agreed to serve as Special Counsel in a politically sensitive investigation involving Governor David Paterson. The issue was straightforward but symbolically important: the Governor had accepted complimentary tickets to Game 1 of the 2009 World Series from the New York Yankees, an organization with extensive interests before the state. Our investigation concluded that the tickets had been actively solicited by his staff, that a backdated check had been created to suggest payment, and that Governor Paterson's testimony about the timing and authorship of that check was inconsistent with the evidence.

I presented the case before the Commission, arguing that the Governor had violated both the Public Officers Law and the Code of Ethics, and recommended an unprecedented $93,000 fine. The Commission ultimately imposed a record $62,000 penalty and referred the matter for potential criminal review. No prosecution followed, but the public message was unmistakable: ethics laws apply equally to everyone, including those who write them. The episode was a reminder that, whatever else I was building in the private sector, my instincts remained the same—accountability and integrity still mattered most.

An Unexpected Pivot

By 2013, another door opened.

The U.S. Department of Justice had entered into a deferred prosecution agreement with HSBC, one of the world's largest banks, over systemic failures in anti-money laundering controls and sanctions compliance, as described in the DOJ's charging documents and deferred prosecution agreement. The agreement required the appointment of an independent corporate monitor—someone who would oversee HSBC's promised reforms and report back to DOJ and global regulators.

This was exactly the kind of work that sat at the crossroads of my world and Mike's: policing institutional behavior without a badge, demanding reform from the inside out, and turning culture change into enforceable practice.

Mike, long gone from Altegrity, called and asked if I would help pursue the assignment with him.

He had the credibility: CEO of a Fortune 100 company, years leading Kroll, and, of course, our LAPD monitorship. I had deep monitorship experience, a methodology for large-scale institutional compliance reviews, and the operational discipline from KeyPoint. We built the pitch together. Mike presented to HSBC, DOJ, and the U.K.'s Financial Services Authority (later split into the FCA and PRA).

It worked. Mike was selected to serve as the independent monitor.

Over breakfast at the Larchmont Diner, while discussing execution, I told him: Don't just be 'the monitor' and farm it out. Build the thing. Stand up a firm that can own this work. Do what was done with Kroll, but do it under your flag.

He did.

Working with Michael Beber, another Kroll alum, Mike formed a new entity—first called Brightline GRC (for Governance, Risk & Compliance) and ultimately rebranded as Exiger. KeyPoint was brought in as one of the support partners. I was named Deputy Monitor for HSBC while still serving as KeyPoint's CEO.

The HSBC work was, in some ways, familiar: assess systems, test compliance, enforce commitments. In other ways, it was unlike anything we had done before. The scale was global. The stakes were geopolitical. We were flying to London, Hong Kong, and Shanghai, meeting with executives whose mistakes could trigger not only an internal investigation but also exposure to international sanctions. We weren't just watching a police department from Figueroa Street. We were watching one of the largest financial institutions on Earth teach itself to obey the law.

For me personally, it was the most complex, high-stakes oversight assignment in which I had ever been involved.

And then—opportunity again knocked.

Veritas, having owned KeyPoint for five years—the typical private equity holding period—began exploring a sale. From an investor's standpoint, the timing was ideal. USIS had largely imploded, but more was to follow. We had absorbed a massive new workload and doubled our investigative workforce to more than 3,000 investigators. Revenue and relevance were both up.

But buyers are not sentimental. A number of potential acquirers looked at KeyPoint and saw a company that had just ingested thousands of new employees in a compressed time frame, with the short-term hit to margins that comes with any surge hire. They balked. Veritas ultimately decided to hold the company.

By that point, though, I had already made a commitment to Cy Vance.

Cy, now Manhattan District Attorney, asked me to come in as his Chief of Staff. It was a chance to return to public service at the highest level of local prosecution, in the very office where I had started my career. I told Veritas I would be leaving. I believed KeyPoint was in capable hands. I also believed—maybe for the first time since I left the DA's Office—that the pull of public work was stronger than the logic of staying where I was.

The story of KeyPoint, at least for me, had reached its inflection point. We had built something consequential, at scale, with integrity. We had outlasted competitors who lost their way. We had proven, at least in our corner of the industry, that you could fully meet government client mandates and, through enhanced efficiency enabled by technology, add to the bottom line.

And at that moment, I understood something that would

define the next chapter of my life: I wasn't done with public service. Not by a long shot.

Chapter 36
A Return to Hogan Place

My decision to re-join the Manhattan DA's Office, was really not a difficult one. KeyPoint was a machine humming smoothly. We had won the battles, defeated our competitors, and stabilized the ship. And there is a specific restlessness that comes with "maintenance mode." I had spent five years building a company, but I had long missed the feeling of doing justice. When the opportunity came to return to One Hogan Place, it wasn't a career step; it was a chance to address issues in the criminal justice system that I had seen from a different vantage point in the private sector. It was a chance to see if the ideals we had developed and honed in the monitorships and various investigations we had undertaken from the private sector could translate productively back into the public sector.

So, in February 2014, shortly after Cy Vance began his second term as Manhattan District Attorney, I returned to the office where I had first learned to practice law—this time not as a line prosecutor, but as its first-ever Chief of Staff. The role, which Cy, Peg, and I conceived together, was loosely modeled on Leo McGarry from The West Wing—the trusted gatekeeper whose judgment, candor, and steadiness kept the White House running. Those were the qualities we hoped the position would bring to One Hogan Place: a center of gravity that could connect policy, people, and principle.

With Dan Alonso stepping down as Chief Assistant, the leadership team was shifting. Karen Friedman-Agnifilo, who, during the initial transition from Morgenthau to Cy, I had recommended for the Chief of Trials position, was being promoted to Chief Assistant. My role was complementary to hers, not hierarchical—designed to manage key initiatives, modernize internal operations, and serve as Cy's strategic advisor on cross-cutting priorities. I also hoped, perhaps idealistically, to recapture the sense of camaraderie and purpose that had defined my early years in the office.

But times—and crime—had changed.

When I left the DA's Office in 1990, New York was still in its bloodiest era, with more than 2,200 murders citywide, over 500 of them in Manhattan alone. The Westies were gone, the Mafia was fading, but the streets were still claimed by narcotics violence. By 2014, the city as a whole recorded only 333 murders—the lowest total in modern history. Yet the criminal landscape hadn't quieted; it had evolved. Financial fraud, cybercrime, public corruption, and transnational money laundering had replaced the mob hits and racketeering cases of old. Prosecutors now needed data scientists as much as detectives. The fight had moved from Hell's Kitchen to the global banking system.

At City Hall, Bill de Blasio had just taken office as mayor, and Bill Bratton was returning as Police Commissioner—this time with a team I knew well: John Miller as Deputy Commissioner for Intelligence and Counterterrorism and John Linder, once again consulting on organizational change. The relationships built across decades of shared work now positioned us for something bigger. Cy and I agreed that it was time for a new model of cooperation between the DA's Office and the NYPD—something beyond coordination, closer to integration. We called it Extreme Collaboration.

Borrowing from Bratton's book *Collaborate or Perish!*, we structured cross-agency working groups, policy councils, and shared reform projects. I chaired the initiative, which soon led to one of the most consequential modernization efforts in NYPD history.

With Deputy Commissioner Jessica Tisch leading the technological side for NYPD, and with Cy's support, we authorized more than $100 million in asset-forfeiture funds to wire every precinct with high-speed internet and equip every patrol officer with a smartphone. It was the largest digital transformation in NYPD's history—laying the groundwork for body-worn cameras, real-time data access, and precinct connectivity that would define the next generation of policing.

I also spearheaded the effort to establish an entity that could serve as a clearinghouse for ideas of prosecutors nationwide. Drawing upon the substantial resources of the Manhattan District Attorney's Office—funds derived from asset forfeitures—we conceived a novel institution to advance the role of prosecutors in an era of reform: the Institute for Innovation in Prosecution (IIP) at John Jay College of Criminal Justice. Working closely with President Jeremy Travis and Cy, we formalized a partnership between the DA's Office and John Jay, creating a national platform dedicated to prosecutor development, data-driven strategy, and the modernization of prosecutorial practice. From the outset, the IIP sought to convene elected DAs, practitioners, scholars, and community stakeholders. Its mission was to elevate the office of the prosecutor not simply as a case-handler, but as an agent of justice, fairness, and innovation. I recommended my friend and former colleague, Meg Reiss, to serve as the Institute's first Executive Director. She got the job.

Around that time, I also answered a call from Mike Feuer, the Los Angeles City Attorney, who wanted to launch a national prosecutorial initiative. Together with Cy and Feuer, we established Prosecutors Against Gun Violence (PAGV), a coalition of major-city prosecutors devoted to reducing gun violence through coordinated policy and enforcement strategies. At our first national summit—held in Atlanta in October 2014—we toured the National Center for Civil and Human Rights, the city's newly opened civil-rights museum. There, I walked with John Lewis, the Georgia Congressman and civil-rights icon, through exhibits of his own activism. A photograph of him showing me a photograph of himself, taken during the movement, remains one of my most prized possessions.

At the same time, New York was still digesting the fallout from Floyd v. City of New York, the 2013 federal decision that found the NYPD's stop-and-frisk practices unconstitutional. The case resulted in a federal settlement requiring sweeping changes to policies, supervision, and documentation. Early in my tenure, I met with the court-appointed monitor, Peter Zimroth, and separately with his deputy, Richard Jerome. I knew Richard from our earlier LAPD work, and though DANY had no formal role in the Floyd monitorship, our discussions on compliance strategy were a professional homecoming of sorts. Years later, when I joined the NYPD, I would return to that very monitorship—no longer as an outside observer, but as the Department's chief liaison to Peter and Richard, helping to implement the reforms we had once analyzed together.

Inside the DA's Office, I also worked to modernize our own identity—literally and figuratively. I pushed for and led the redesign of the office's re-branding, introducing a clean new logo and visual presentation that reflected professionalism and progress. It may have seemed cosmetic, but the change carried symbolic weight: an acknowledgment that the institution could evolve while honoring its legacy. Newly branded coffee mugs and T-shirts sold out.

Cy's first term had already been defined by cases that tested the balance between prosecutorial restraint and public expectation. The Dominique Strauss-Kahn case was one. In 2011, the head of the International Monetary Fund was accused of sexual assault by a hotel housekeeper. DNA evidence and medical findings initially appeared damning. But as the case progressed, questions arose—as reflected in the Office's public filings and contemporaneous reporting—about the accuser's credibility, including statements later determined to be false on her asylum application, conflicting accounts she gave about portions of the incident, and a recorded conversation that was interpreted as reflecting potential financial motives. After exhaustive internal debate, Cy made the difficult decision to dismiss the case. It was not necessarily popular, but it was, in my view, the correct decision. The duty of a prosecutor is not to win, but to be certain—and when certainty evaporates, ethics require that you stop.

Another matter, quieter but in hindsight more consequential, was the 2012 investigation into the Trump SoHo real estate project. As reported in the press, there were allegations that Donald Trump Jr. and Ivanka Trump had exaggerated condominium sales figures to attract investors—conduct that, if proven, could have constituted felony fraud. After reviewing the evidence, the Office concluded that the proof was insufficient to sustain a conviction.

Throughout my career, I'd believed that transparency of process to the public was important. I urged that the DA's Office formalize and publicly articulate its threshold for prosecution—requiring an internal certainty of guilt, evidence sufficient to establish probable cause that a crime was committed, and a reasonable, though not certain, likelihood that a jury would convict. The purpose was not to constrain discretion, but to make transparent the reasoning behind it.

After sixteen months as Chief of Staff, I decided to step down. I had accomplished much of what I set out to do—strengthening the partnership with the NYPD and modernizing systems. But I also realized that eras can't be recreated. The office I returned to was not the one I had left decades earlier, and that was as it should be. Still, the pulse of purpose that had drawn me to public service in the first place remained strong.

When I discussed my decision with Cherkasky, he asked me to join Exiger—which was expanding rapidly on the heels of the HSBC monitorship. The timing felt right. I left the DA's Office grateful and renewed.

After I left, I remained very closely connected to Cy and the work we had begun. Through the end of his three terms, we'd have dinner once a week, talking through everything from policy reforms to the latest headlines that touched the criminal justice system. Those evenings reminded me of why I had come back in the first place: to think boldly, to challenge assumptions, and to keep searching for ways to make the system more just, more transparent, and more humane.

Chapter 37
A Global Watchdog

When I left the DA's Office to rejoin Mike at Exiger, it wasn't just a reunion. It was a bet—on him, on a new company, on myself, and on a model of oversight we believed could scale globally.

To bring me in, Mike offered me an equity stake in the firm, vesting over five years, and asked me to serve as President of the Advisory Group. The Advisory Group was the heart of the company at that early stage. It encompassed not only the HSBC monitorship—the assignment that had given birth to Exiger—but also a broader practice advising international banks and financial institutions on anti-money-laundering (AML), sanctions compliance, and organizational ethics.

At the beginning, the HSBC monitorship wasn't just a client. It was the company.

HSBC had entered into a settlement with the U.S. Department of Justice after years of systemic anti-money-laundering failures, including allowing drug cartel proceeds to move through its accounts and processing transactions in violation of U.S. sanctions. Our job as monitors was to evaluate and enforce the bank's promised reforms. The scale of that work was unlike anything I had done before: teams on the ground in London, Hong Kong, the Middle East, Latin America, and New York; deep dives into transaction-monitoring systems and "Know Your Customer" controls; and cultural assessments of whether "compliance" meant anything beyond a slide deck. We weren't just checking boxes. We were, in effect, helping a global bank rebuild its internal immune system.

By the time I arrived, Exiger envisioned three main business lines: (1) the Advisory Group, which I was running; (2) a due diligence practice; and (3) a fledgling technology solutions arm.

That third line—tech—was the one that would ultimately change everything.

At that point, Exiger didn't actually own the core technology it was selling to clients. We were relying heavily on a tool called DDIQ to automate diligence and compliance checks, in which Exiger owned a minority stake. I had lived through the danger of that kind of dependency at KeyPoint. After my government services business spun out of Kroll, a sister company called Kroll Factual Data was still providing automated data for our TSA vetting work. When that sister company later fell under the control of Altegrity, they simply cut us off. It nearly crippled a major line of business. I told Mike that if Exiger didn't own its technology outright, we would always be at risk. He listened and moved to secure full control of DDIQ. That decision is one of the reasons Exiger was later sold for a reported $1.3 billion.

But I didn't view Exiger as only a bank-compliance shop. I saw the opportunity to build out a government-oversight and public-sector practice that would stand alongside the private-sector work—and, in time, feed the technology strategy.

I reached out to Chris Prather, a former colleague from the Manhattan DA's Office who had gone on to K2 (the firm started by Jules and Jeremy Kroll after Kroll was sold). Chris agreed to join Exiger, and together, we built a construction-monitoring practice: essentially, independent oversight of large public and quasi-public infrastructure projects to prevent fraud, cost abuse, and security failures. It grew faster than I expected. It was proof that the Exiger model—independence plus rigor plus relentless documentation—wasn't just something banks would buy.

To support the expansion, I recruited Brad Breslin from K2, who became my Chief of Staff. I also brought over Victor Cabrera, my longtime assistant, who had been with me through KeyPoint and the DA's Office and now followed me to Exiger.

Our London office became a second operational hub. It housed people who were as valuable as our U.S. leadership. Vesna

McCreery, who had previously led AML functions at Barclays, brought credibility with British and European regulators. Lisa Osofsky ran the London practice; she had a remarkable pedigree, including work with the FBI, time at Decision Strategies (one of Kroll's competitors), and would go on to become Director of the U.K.'s Serious Fraud Office.

And with us in New York, there was Arun Banerjee, the most effective seller and closer of high-stakes advisory work I've ever seen. Arun had that rare ability to understand client anxiety, turn it into a concrete scope, and then get the client to sign a check for the work. He helped take us from "you're the HSBC people" to "you're the ones we call when we cannot afford to fail."

Even with HSBC dominating the agenda, I took on two major matters that signaled an important direction in which I wanted Exiger to expand—into independent expert assessments and monitorships across multiple disciplines.

One was in Cincinnati.

Reforming a Police Department in Real Time

On July 19, 2015, a University of Cincinnati Police Division (UCPD) officer named Ray Tensing stopped a car just off campus for a missing front plate. The driver, Samuel DuBose, an unarmed Black man, was shot in the head at point-blank range. The killing—captured on Tensing's body camera—ignited outrage in Cincinnati and far beyond. The Hamilton County prosecutor called the shooting "senseless" and indicted Tensing for murder and voluntary manslaughter. Meanwhile, the University of Cincinnati found itself facing not just a scandal, but an existential crisis: Did a campus police officer, patrolling off campus, escalate a traffic stop for a minor violation into a fatal shooting? And if so, why?

An initial report by colleagues I had left behind at Kroll concluded, bluntly, that the shooting was "entirely preventable." The problems, they found, weren't limited to one officer. UCPD had adopted an aggressive traffic-stop culture under its leadership at the time—a surge in enforcement, especially against Black motorists, far from campus, on vaguely articulated public safety grounds. Oversight had been lax. Training had been shallow. The mission had drifted.

That's when the University brought us in.

In January 2016, a team that I had put together and led was hired to do a full structural review of UCPD. The 12-person team included national policing heavyweights: former Philadelphia Police Commissioner Charles Ramsey; former Tucson Police Chief Roberto Villaseñor, known to everyone as Taz; and a number of former LAPD alumni who had gone on into consulting. Denise Lewis, whom I first met years earlier when she was a sergeant in LAPD's Audit Unit and who later worked with me at Kroll, KeyPoint, Exiger, and IntegrAssure, was also on the team. Our mandate was not just to analyze what happened the night DuBose was shot, but to tell the University—candidly—what was broken, who was responsible, and how to fix it.

Our review found that UCPD's leadership had chased street-policing credibility it was not built to exercise. Traffic stops had tripled. The stops fell disproportionately on Black motorists. Officers were acting as if they were a municipal enforcement unit, not a campus safety agency. Our review concluded that the chief and a senior commander had downplayed these trends in their communications with university leadership. The system was drifting toward danger, and no one in authority had hit the brakes.

Our June 2016 report pulled no punches. It called for 276 specific reforms: use-of-force policy overhaul, bias-free policing standards, rewritten mission and jurisdictional limits, complaint and discipline reforms, de-escalation training, body-worn and in-car cameras, revised recruitment and supervision, and leadership change. Two members of the leadership team ultimately left their positions as part of the reforms that followed.

Then something remarkable happened.

Rather than resist, the University of Cincinnati, under the expert guidance of noted criminologist Robin Engel, who had been elevated from her teaching role to Vice President for Public Safety, voluntarily agreed to monitored reform. On November 1, 2016, UC appointed me as Independent Monitor, with Taz as my Deputy Monitor and my Exiger team providing support. We reported publicly and tracked implementation of the recommended reforms. We met with community stakeholders. We pushed, but we also helped, providing technical support across a wide range of reform areas. Denise and Taz stayed with the project when I left to join the NYPD in 2018. By 2019, every one of the 276 recommendations had been implemented. UCPD didn't just "clean up a mess." It rewrote its identity: from an enforcement-heavy traffic-stop engine to a community safety agency with a defined scope, transparent rules, and actual accountability.

The DuBose family did not get the criminal closure they sought; two trials of the officer ended in hung juries. A later settlement with the officer over back pay infuriated the community. Reform doesn't undo a death. But structurally? UCPD became a national example of what campus policing can and should look like. I stayed in touch with the leaders who drove that change—Robin; Jim Whalen, a former Cincinnati Police Chief who helped stabilize operations; and Maris Herold, who assumed the UCPD chief role and would go on to lead the Boulder, Colorado, Police Department. They did not treat the "monitorship" as a burden. They treated it as fulfilling an obligation to make the department the best it could be.

In the end, that is all one can reasonably ask.

Nuevo León

In 2017, I was in Monterrey, in the state of Nuevo León, Mexico, sitting across from business leaders, police commanders, and government officials whose core concern wasn't compliance frameworks or reputational risk. It was staying alive.

Nuevo León was being squeezed by organized crime: gun violence, kidnappings, extortion, and targeted assassinations. The state's private sector—the industrial and logistics engine of northern Mexico—understood something that sometimes takes U.S. cities years to admit: if you lose public safety, you lose everything else.

Bill Bratton got the initial call and sent it my way. We met with the head of the state chamber of commerce, the governor, and the public safety secretary. I built a team to address the issues facing Nuevo León: Dan Alonso and Eli Cherkasky from Exiger; and, critically, Lou Anemone, who had been Chief of Department at the NYPD during the 1990s and who, in that role, was among the drivers of the famed CompStat process. Lou brought two Spanish-speaking former NYPD detectives with him. The assignment was blunt: help us get control.

What we found in Nuevo León was a familiar pathology in a new setting. Law enforcement agencies worked in silos. They chased individual categories of crime—narcotics, robberies, kidnappings—like separate fiefdoms. No one owned geography.

We pushed to flip that model. Instead of saying "this is a drug problem" or "this is a kidnapping problem," we said, "this is a hot zone," and treated violence as a place-based phenomenon. That approach—geographic hot-spot policing combined with rapid accountability—is what had helped drive New York City's violent crime down years earlier. But to make it work in Nuevo León, where corruption and fear were constant factors, we had to build something else alongside it: accountability structures.

So we brought in CompStat.

CompStat, in its original NYPD form, was more than a meeting. It was a culture of forced clarity: What happened? Where? Who is responsible for fixing it? What have you done since last week? Show me. Under Lou Anemone's guidance, we customized it for Monterrey and surrounding municipalities. We ran joint sessions with state and municipal leadership, and we forced agencies that barely spoke to each other to sit at the same table and answer for results.

The first real CompStat session in Nuevo León is something I still remember. You could feel the discomfort. You could also feel the electricity. Suddenly, tactical decisions weren't buried inside different chains of command; they were on a table, in public, with maps. You could watch the room understand, in real time, that "coordination" wasn't a slogan—it was survival.

We also dealt directly with the private sector. In Nuevo León, unlike in most American cities, the business community wasn't just a donor class or an advisory group. They were partners. They understood that safer streets meant more foreign investment, fewer kidnappings of executives, and more stability for the workforce. They had leverage, and they used it—in the right direction.

Was the work easy? No. Corruption, political turnover, pressure from organized criminal groups—all of that pushed against progress every day. But we left them with a framework: focus on geography, measure performance, demand coordination, and treat public safety as infrastructure, not theater. It wasn't a Hollywood ending. It was, hopefully, the beginning of a habit.

The Exit

For all the meaningful work we accomplished, my time at Exiger eventually ran its natural course. From the beginning, Mike had built the company in partnership with Michael Beber, a structure that was both generous and forward-thinking—with 51 percent held between them and 49 percent reserved for employees. It was designed to foster shared ownership and long-term commitment, and it did exactly that.

By 2018, it was clear that Beber and I had different management styles and different ways of interacting with people, including each other. At the same time, an exciting new opportunity was emerging—one that would allow me to return to public service. After three years of building and leading the Advisory Group, recruiting and mentoring a strong team, and expanding our global reach, I decided it was time to step away.

I maintained an investment in the company—a gesture of continued belief in the mission and the people who had helped build it. When Exiger later sold, it was clear that my confidence was well placed.

It was a fitting conclusion: playing a formative role in a successful enterprise standing on its own, and a personal reminder that leadership sometimes means knowing when to move on.

On April 6, 2018, I left Exiger. I took one week—my first without a job since 1978—and on April 16, I reported for duty at the NYPD.

Chapter 38
Inside the Machine

My path into the NYPD started, as so many turns in my career did, with a dinner. I had done what I'd come to Exiger to do, and given my displeasure with the internal dynamic at the top and the fact that I could afford to go back into public service, it just did not make sense to stay. And I still believed—maybe stubbornly—that large institutions like NYPD could be made better if the right pressure was put in the right place.

It was at dinner that two old allies pushed me to join them at One Police Plaza: John Linder, who I knew from our LAPD consent decree years and whom I had been seeing regularly since he began his NYPD consulting work with Bill Bratton's second stint as Commissioner, and John Miller, whom I'd first become acquainted with in the Gotti days and then again in Los Angeles. John was serving as the Deputy Commissioner for Intelligence and Counterterrorism at the NYPD. Bratton had already stepped down and moved back to the private sector. I had always hoped to work directly under Bill inside the NYPD. That window had closed. But the draw of working with old friends in the storied institution that I had, for years, admired from a distance was almost irresistible.

When Bratton resigned in September 2016, he handed the reins to his Chief of Department, James O'Neill. O'Neill inherited an NYPD under intense strain. The department was carrying two open wounds: the Eric Garner case and a corruption scandal centered around Jonah Rechnitz and Jeremy Reichberg, who had allegedly plied senior NYPD officials with trips, escorts, and luxury gifts.

The Garner case had ignited national outrage and become a symbol of racialized policing.

The Rechnitz/Reichberg scandal cut in a different way: it exposed access-buying and favoritism at the highest levels of the

Department. Bratton had moved quickly—forcing out Phil Banks as Chief of Department, tightening gift rules, modernizing training and discipline—but by the time O'Neill took over, there was still a question hanging over the NYPD: could it actually police itself?

Linder set up a lunch between O'Neill and me. I knew O'Neill from when he was Chief of Department, but we hadn't worked together. He seemed to want someone who could help manage reform, deal with court oversight, and talk plainly about risk. I certainly wanted to do all those things.

I accepted the job as Counsel to the Police Commissioner. It carried a three-star rank. The thought—at least from Linder and Miller—was that I would eventually move into the role of Deputy Commissioner of Legal Matters when Larry Byrne left. Larry, whom I'd known for years and respected personally, had shaped DCLM as a classic institutional defense shop: protect the department, control exposure, fight outsiders. I had no interest in that. I wasn't coming in to rationalize past behavior. I was coming in to help change future behavior.

That, as I quickly learned, was easier said than done.

The Shadow of Eric Garner

In order to understand what I tried to build inside the NYPD, an understanding of what was hanging over the Department is necessary.

Eric Garner's death in July 2014 was one of those moments that reorganize the public conversation. Garner, a 43-year-old Staten Island resident, was taken to the ground by Officer Daniel Pantaleo during an arrest for allegedly selling untaxed cigarettes. Pantaleo allegedly used what was, by NYPD policy, a banned chokehold. Garner said, "I can't breathe," again and again while officers kept him pinned.

The whole thing was on video.

When a Staten Island grand jury declined to indict Pantaleo, it wasn't just a local controversy. It broke open an argument about policing and race in America that would reverberate for years. "I can't breathe" became a national chant. And for those of us who had spent our lives somewhere between cops and communities, it carried a different kind of weight. It said: this isn't just about whether force was technically "authorized." It's about whether anyone in power is willing to say out loud that what happened was wrong.

The Garner case followed O'Neill into office like a ghost. It never left. The federal civil-rights review dragged. The NYPD disciplinary case against Pantaleo sat unresolved. Garner's family demanded action. The rank and file demanded protection. Every move was radioactive.

That unresolved pressure sat in every room I walked into at One Police Plaza. It set the stakes for reform. It also hardened resistance to reform. You could feel both.

David Floyd v. City of New York

On top of Garner, the department was under a court-ordered mandates for reform.

When I started at the NYPD on April 16, 2018, the City was still living under the consequences of David Floyd v. City of New York, the landmark federal case that found NYPD's stop-and-frisk practices unconstitutional. Judge Shira Scheindlin's 2013 opinion was devastating. She found that NYPD's stop activity violated both the Fourth and Fourteenth Amendments, that there were racial disparities built into the way stops were conducted and recorded, and that officers were being pushed—explicitly or implicitly—to "get their numbers up."

That case had two aspects that the LAPD litigation hadn't.

First, it was brought by private plaintiffs in a class action lawsuit. Second, it went to trial. The LAPD case had been brought by DOJ, and Los Angeles agreed to DOJ-mandated oversight without a trial. New York decided to fight, lost in open court, and had its conduct spelled out in a 198-page ruling for the world to read.

The post-trial settlement agreement was negotiated between the new de Blasio administration and the plaintiffs after the decision. The City dropped the Bloomberg-era appeal, accepted the findings, and agreed to sweeping reforms: rewrite stop documentation, retrain officers, build supervisory accountability, pilot body-worn cameras, and submit to an independent federal monitor.

Judge Scheindlin appointed Peter Zimroth as that monitor. Peter had been Chief Assistant District Attorney in Manhattan before my time, later Corporation Counsel for the City, and then a law-firm partner and professor. His deputy was Richard Jerome, whom I knew well, following our initial encounter at DOJ when he told us about the pending monitorship in Los Angeles and our intermittent crossing of paths.

Between 2014 and 2018, Peter's team issued report after report. Stops dropped dramatically. Policies were rewritten. Body-worn cameras rolled out. But there were still glaring problems: inconsistent supervision, weak follow-through, and chronic underreporting of stops that still happened but were never logged.

Inside the NYPD, the Floyd monitorship had been assigned to an Assistant Commissioner named Nancy Hoppock. She reported first to Larry Byrne, then—after tensions between Byrne and the Monitor turned toxic—to First Deputy Commissioner Ben Tucker.

Ben Tucker is worth pausing on. He had come up through the NYPD in the 1970s, gone to law school at night, held senior roles in DOJ and in the Clinton White House drug-policy office, and then returned under Bratton in 2014 as First Deputy Commissioner. Ben was exactly what you want in that job: calm, principled, allergic to drama, and quietly relentless. Alongside him was Chief Matt Pontillo, one of the smartest cops I've ever worked with.

Those two became essential allies.

The Risk Management Bureau

A few months into my tenure as Counsel to the Commissioner, Hoppock departed to become Chief Assistant District Attorney at the Brooklyn District Attorney's Office. I was asked to assume her responsibilities. I agreed—but only on two conditions.

First, the work had to be elevated. Risk management could not be treated as a compliance sideline or a box-checking exercise. If the Department was serious about reform, then reform required real authority, clear ownership, and institutional standing. Second, it needed structure. I was not interested in inheriting a "unit" buried inside another command. Risk management deserved to stand on its own. The Commissioner agreed.

I was appointed the first Deputy Commissioner of the newly created Risk Management Bureau—a three-star position. It marked the first time the NYPD had placed the word "risk" in the title of a bureau. That was not a semantic change; it was a statement of intent. The Bureau's mission was blunt by design: to ask what the Department was doing that might get someone killed, get the City sued, or place the NYPD under an even heavier court order five years down the road—and then to fix it before we were forced to explain later that we "never saw it coming."

One of my earliest priorities relative to the Monitorship was to press Peter Zimroth to do in New York what we had done in Los Angeles: define compliance in plain English. In L.A. we had developed a common yardstick—clear methodologies for determining compliance—so that neither the Department nor the Monitor could later argue about what "substantial compliance" meant. I proposed the same approach in New York. Working with the Monitor's team, we set the goalposts. That, in itself, was a meaningful accomplishment.

Yet defining compliance and achieving it are not the same thing. As of this writing in 2026—more than a decade later—the

Department has not moved the ball through the uprights. The NYPD remains under federal court oversight, still struggling to substantially comply with the Court's orders. Zimroth passed away in November 2021, and while a new Monitor has since been appointed, Richard Jerome and much of the team I worked with remain in place—a reminder of how durable these institutional failures can be once they take root.

The Monitorship, however, was only one part of what landed on my desk when the Risk Management Bureau was created.

Beyond the federal monitorship, the Risk Management Bureau, as I viewed it and shaped it, was meant to function as the Department's internal early-warning and course-correction mechanism. It integrated disparate existing functions including compliance oversight, performance monitoring, data integrity, internal audits, litigation analysis, and officer-risk assessment into a single enterprise-wide function, while also serving as the Department's principal liaison to external oversight bodies, including the Inspector General. The Bureau's charge was straightforward but ambitious: identify emerging risks, translate them into concrete reforms, test whether those reforms worked, and intervene early—before failures hardened into tragedy, scandal, or court order.

The work did not make me popular.

The first resistance came, predictably, from within. There were still powerful voices both in Legal and in the traditional command structure—who viewed "reform" not as improvement but as an existential threat. Some of that resistance was cultural; some of it was plainly self-protective. Early on, a one-star chief who reported to me made it clear, mostly through posture rather than words, that he regarded me as an outsider who needed to be watched. He was hardly alone.

That said, there were also senior leaders inside the command structure who understood exactly what we were trying to do—even as they, too, were pushing against an entrenched mindset. Isa

Abassi and Fausto Pichardo saw risk management not as a challenge to authority but as a means of preserving it. And throughout, I had steadfast allies in Ben Tucker and Matt Pontillo, whose support reflected a shared belief that the Department's future depended on its willingness to confront its risks honestly.

Over time, I was able to build a team that believed in the work. At the inception, I was deliberate in seeking out and elevating those who I believed understood reform not as surrender but as professional obligation—people like Lt. Renee Appelbaum, Det. Marlene Perez, and Capt. Ari Maas, all who proved to be thoughtful, pragmatic, and aligned in the belief that institutional credibility depended on doing the work honestly. They became trusted allies, not because they agreed with every conclusion, but because they were committed to the premise that the department would be stronger—not weaker—if it was willing to look squarely at itself.

I fought for, and secured, the appointment of a civilian two-star to anchor major initiatives. That was Erin Pilnyak, a former Manhattan ADA and a gifted project manager, with the credibility and discipline to move complex work forward across entrenched silos. I also recruited Inspector Mark Iocco, who understood what real risk management looks like inside a police department—not as theory, but as practice.

The Pantaleo Decision

Although the Garner case did not fall within the direct ambit of my Bureau, it sat at the intersection of the very risks and institutional challenges the Risk Management Bureau was created to confront. The case which had lingered for more than five years needed to be resolved.

In June 2019, a disciplinary trial concluded with Administrative Law Judge Rosemarie Maldonado recommending that Officer Daniel Pantaleo be fired for using a banned chokehold that led to Eric Garner's death. On August 19, 2019, Commissioner O'Neill announced Pantaleo's termination.

O'Neill said, publicly, that the decision had "weighed on him" and that he believed it was the right call. The Garner family and civil rights advocates called it overdue justice. The Police Benevolent Association declared a vote of no confidence in O'Neill and said he had "lost the department."

You could feel the ground shift that day. Internally, it was clear that O'Neill understood the moral stakes. It was also clear that the decision isolated him. A few months later, in December 2019, he resigned and moved into the private sector. Mayor de Blasio chose Dermot Shea, then Chief of Detectives, to succeed him over First Deputy Commissioner Ben Tucker.

I very much liked Dermot personally. He was smart, direct, and knew the NYPD from the sidewalk up. But by then I had learned a painful truth: when you elevate only people who have spent their entire lives inside an organization, you get continuity. You rarely get transformation. The NYPD was an insular organization that viewed itself as setting the standard for policing. In many ways, it did. But it also didn't know what it didn't know.

My concern was simple. The department was under court order. Public trust was collapsing. I thought we needed someone who could look at the place from the outside, even while sitting on the inside. This was the recipe that Bill Bratton had brought to both New York and Los Angeles.

Early Intervention

One of the things we did as an outgrowth of the monitorship was to create an Early Intervention Program meant to surface officers who were showing patterns of potentially problematic behavior—not necessarily for discipline, but for examination and, if needed, remediation through coaching, mentoring, training, and enhanced supervision.

We instituted standing "RISKS Reviews." RISKS was an acronym for Remediation of Identified Situations Key to Success. We would sit down with a command, walk through their data, their stops, their body-worn camera usage, and their paperwork, and ask the uncomfortable questions. We didn't just count stops; we watched them. We pulled body-worn camera footage and reviewed it for legality and professionalism. We did this with all 78 commands in the City on a rotating basis.

That work led us to one of the most consequential findings of my time at the NYPD.

What Anti-Crime Was Really Doing

Every NYPD precinct had an Anti-Crime Unit: a small plainclothes team whose job was to hunt guns, robbers, and violent offenders before they struck. In theory, they were proactive crime-suppression units. In practice, from what we saw, some had evolved into high-discretion stop squads with light supervision and even lighter documentation.

Five years after the Floyd ruling, we were still seeing widespread underreporting of stops—not just bad paperwork, but stops that were never recorded at all. We were seeing body-worn cameras not activated or activated late. We were seeing tactics that pushed past legal thresholds. And we were seeing serious racial disparities. This wasn't hypothetical. It showed up in the footage.

The Monitor hadn't focused on Anti-Crime as a distinct problem set. We did.

Commissioner Shea asked me a fair question: Could you show, down to the hour, what actually happens in a precinct, and more specifically with the Anti-Crime Unit? In essence, a day in the life.

In the midst of the pandemic, working with one of the quiet heroes of the NYPD, Police Officer David Kaen—who, without exaggeration, could out-analyze most professional data scientists—we built what became the Detailed Analysis of Tour Activity, or D.A.T.A. Analysis. We aligned case activity, stop records, arrest data, radio runs, and body-worn camera metadata on a chronological timeline. You could sit with a command and say: at

14:37 hours, your Anti-Crime team made contact with X. Show me the stop report. Show me the body-worn camera video. Show me the justification.

With Dave's data analysis in hand, we undertook a deep-dive review of BWC video. What we saw in some Anti-Crime Units was, in our judgment, indefensible. Cameras off when they should have been on. Stops never documented. Questionable legal bases for intrusions. Patterns that would, in any courtroom, shred an officer's credibility.

When we briefed Shea in mid-June 2020—with First Deputy Commissioner Ben Tucker, Chief of Patrol Fausto Pichardo, Deputy Commissioner Chauncey Parker, Chief Iocco, and Chief Pontillo in the room—I told him plainly: this isn't just a civil risk. It's personal exposure. Officers could face prosecutorial jeopardy if they continued like this. And the department would lose the last of its credibility on constitutional policing if we didn't act.

Three days later, Shea announced the disbanding of NYPD's Anti-Crime Units citywide.

That call was his. To his credit, it was bold. Our recommendations had been more incremental: move the officers into uniform, tighten supervision, enforce body-worn camera activation, mandate documentation, increase training. Shea chose to go further. He understood the moment. It was June 2020. The city was in the streets after the murder of George Floyd. The moral tolerance for "cowboy policing" had hit zero.

Inside the department, that decision was met in some quarters with disdain. Some said the sky would fall. Others claimed we'd just "tied the hands" of the cops stopping shootings. I understood the anger. I also knew the alternative was worse. You cannot tell communities you are committed to constitutional policing and then keep in place units whose day-to-day practices cannot survive daylight.

The Matrix

While we were tackling stop activity, we were also working on another fault line: discipline.

For years, discipline inside the NYPD had been criticized as inconsistent, opaque, and political. Officers and the public both believed that rank mattered more than conduct. In 2018 and 2019, an outside panel convened by Commissioner O'Neill—led by former U.S. Attorneys Mary Jo White and Rob Capers, and former federal judge Barbara Jones—recommended creating a formal disciplinary matrix. I had only a passing acquaintance with Mary Jo White and Rob Capers, but I knew Barbara well—from her days in the U.S. Attorney's Office under Rudolph Giuliani, through our chance meeting outside Sparks at the Castellano shooting scene, and later, far more closely, after she joined the Manhattan District Attorney's Office as Chief Assistant. The idea of a disciplinary matrix was simple: define presumptive penalties for specific violations, allow for aggravating and mitigating factors, and require the Commissioner to justify any deviation.

Matt Pontillo and I worked side by side to turn that recommendation into something real. The point was not to take discretion away from the Commissioner. The point was to drag discretion into the light. If you're going to cut a penalty in half, say why. If you're going to increase it, say why. Put it in writing. Let the officer see it. Let the public see it.

In a department that had, for generations, resisted outside scrutiny of discipline—aided in part by New York Civil Rights Law § 50-a, which for years kept officer discipline records secret—this was a cultural break. It said: accountability is not a betrayal of the job. It is part of the job.

This was the world we were trying to build from inside.

And then the outside world broke.

Chapter 39
Crisis Stacking

In March 2020, before the murder of George Floyd, before the protests, before the political knives fully came out, COVID hit New York City and tore through the NYPD.

The department logged its first confirmed COVID case on March 12, 2020. Within weeks, nearly one in five officers was out sick. More than 1,900 members had tested positive by early April. At the peak, some precincts had nearly a third of their people unavailable.

The first NYPD employee to die from the virus was Dennis Dickson, a custodial assistant who had quietly taken care of One Police Plaza for fourteen years. Soon after, Detective Cedric Dixon from the 32nd Precinct in Harlem became the first sworn member to die. Later, Chief Bill Morris, the three-star Chief of Personnel who had sworn me in, died after nearly four decades on the job, becoming the highest-ranking member of the Department to die. By the time the first wave subsided, the department had lost more than sixty members—sworn and civilian.

COVID didn't care about rank, command, medals, or bravado. It simply moved.

Inside the department, there was denial at first. Dr. Eli Kleinman, the NYPD's Chief Surgeon, warned early that this thing would rip through the workforce unless masking and distancing were enforced. Those warnings were initially brushed off. Only after the first deaths—and after Commissioner Dermot Shea himself began wearing a mask in command meetings—did the culture shift. Even then, compliance was uneven and often political. Later, when vaccines became available and the City pushed hard on mandates, resistance flared again—this time wrapped in rhetoric about freedom and loyalty. Public health had become a loyalty test.

COVID twisted policing in other ways too. Officers, who had signed up to chase felons and answer 911 calls, were suddenly asked to enforce mask orders and social distancing. Unsurprisingly, that enforcement wasn't always even. Report after report showed racial disparities in early "social distancing arrests," especially in Brooklyn. Meanwhile, Rikers Island was on fire with infection, and hundreds of detainees were released to reduce density—a public health necessity that nonetheless fed a political narrative that "the city had gone soft." It was a no-win posture: enforce and you were accused of over-policing; don't enforce and you were accused of abandoning order.

And while the overall index crime dipped during the first lockdown, shootings and homicides later rose and stayed elevated for years beyond 2020. Everyone, inside and outside government, argued about why. No one could deny that the system was under strain.

Then, as the department was still bleeding from COVID, George Floyd was murdered in Minneapolis.

From David Floyd to George Floyd

On May 25, 2020, Derek Chauvin knelt on George Floyd's neck for more than nine minutes while Floyd said, "I can't breathe," and while bystanders begged officers to stop.

If Eric Garner had exposed the fracture, George Floyd ripped it wide open.

What had been rage in 2014 became something closer to an existential demand in 2020. You could feel that this wasn't just a protest. It was an indictment.

From inside the NYPD, you saw multiple truths colliding at once.

On the street, there were peaceful marches with a disciplined message and moral clarity. There were also nights of confrontation: smashed glass, thrown bottles, burned vehicles, and, in some instances, police responses that escalated rather than calmed. The scale, intensity, and relentlessness of those first ten days were unlike anything the department had seen since the late 1960s.

Inside commands, officers were exhausted, angry, defensive, grieving, and in some cases quietly ashamed. Many felt that the public no longer distinguished between Derek Chauvin and every other cop in America. Others felt abandoned by City Hall. Still others understood perfectly well why people were in the street—and quietly agreed with them. I remember moments of grace in that period—an officer passing bottled water to protesters in 90-degree heat, officers kneeling alongside marchers, a young woman stopping to thank a cop for keeping his cool while he was being screamed at. They were small moments, but they mattered. They reminded me that legitimacy is not an abstract word. You either earn it in real time or you lose it.

Politically, the fallout hardened into policy almost overnight. On June 12, 2020, Governor Andrew Cuomo issued Executive Order 203, requiring every police department in New York State to conduct a public-facing review of its policies, community relationships, and use-of-force practices, and to adopt a reform plan in consultation with the community. At the NYPD, I helped staff and shape that response. We convened stakeholder meetings, opened ourselves—at least nominally—to public comment, and documented proposed changes.

Much of the rank-and-file saw EO 203 as political theater—a box-checking exercise. But two things can be true. Yes, it had politics all over it. And yes, it also forced police departments to do something they rarely do willingly: sit down, in daylight, and explain themselves to the people they police.

Leaving

By early 2021, after three years inside, I felt two things at once.

The first was pride. We had built the Risk Management Bureau and given it real weight. We had forced uncomfortable conversations about stops, body-worn cameras, and documentation. We had exposed, with data and video, practices that could not survive scrutiny. We had created an Early Intervention Program. We had built the D.A.T.A. model, which I still use and refine to this day. We had worked with Pontillo to hammer discipline into a matrix that the public could actually understand. We had pushed the department, sometimes dragging it, toward the idea that integrity is not a talking point—but an operational necessity.

The second was clarity. The institution was starting to push back.

Quietly, there were discussions about collapsing the Risk Management Bureau back under the Legal Bureau. That was not a bureaucratic footnote. It was a philosophical reversal. Risk Management, as we built it, asked, "What are we doing wrong, and how do we fix it before someone gets hurt or we end up under an even broader mandate?" The Legal Bureau's traditional posture was, "How do we shield the Department from liability?" Those are not the same mission. In fact, at times, they are in direct conflict.

That tension surfaced in a debate over whether the Bureau should proactively request referrals of at-risk officers for non-disciplinary intervention. To me, the answer was obvious: of course, we should. To some others, the answer was equally obvious: absolutely not—that creates discoverable material that could be used against us in court. That told me everything.

I didn't want my departure to turn into a symbolic fight. I didn't want to torch the place on the way out. I wanted the Bureau to survive. I hoped that, with me gone, the work might be allowed to continue quietly.

In mid-February 2021, I submitted my resignation letter to Commissioner Shea. In it, I tried to be both respectful and blunt:

> Commissioner:
>
> It is with mixed emotions that I inform you that I intend to resign from my position with the Department as of March 19, 2021. It has been an honor to be a Member of the Service and to serve under you and Commissioner Tucker as the Deputy Commissioner of the Risk Management Bureau (RMB).
>
> RMB is a piece of the Department which for too long had been missing. Its creation filled a gap in the Department by devoting, at the Bureau level, resources to identify and remediate the very formidable risks the Department faces. After a professional career largely focused on police reform, it has been my goal since joining the Department to help fulfill the continuous improvement commitment that underlies the Department's approach since 2014. I thought that I could best help by working from within the Department. Indeed, because of the dedication and hard work of RMB personnel, the Risk Management Bureau has had truly significant achievements during my tenure.
>
> With these accomplishments, I believe the time has come when I can now accomplish more from outside the Department than from within. Given the continued challenges that we face, I thought it would be helpful to provide my thoughts on the steps that I believe are necessary to fully restore the public's faith in its police department; to restore the shine to what has, from a large segment of the public's perspective, become our tarnished shields. By doing so, we will not only ultimately gain the trust of the community and from them the respect and admiration that the vast, vast majority of our members so richly deserve, but will restore the morale and pride of our members which for far too long has been significantly diminished.

First and foremost, we must acknowledge what has gone wrong with the Department over its history and apologize for the role NYPD has played in the perpetuation of unequal treatment of people of color—both residents of our great City and our own members of the service.

As a wise friend of mine has said, the fish in the aquarium don't see the water. We must now both see the water and refill the tank. It is critical that we go further than we have: it is not enough to be non-racist; we must be anti-racist; it is not enough to address implicit biases in the Department, we must actively seek out those with explicit biases, and do everything we can to purge them from our ranks.

We must double down on abiding by the well-established principles of modern policing outlined by Sir Robert Peel and operate strictly and unwaveringly within the rule-of-law foundation provided by the U.S. Constitution and federal, state and city law. We must ensure that there are never winks or nods to those who disregard those standards for achieving what they might believe is a higher purpose of fighting crime. Simply put, if crime-fighting can't be done 100 percent legally, we shouldn't be employing that tactic.

We must make integrity the north star of our Department, where every officer understands the basic tenets of what is required of NYPD members of the service. The consequences for violating those tenets must be swift and certain.

[W]e must delve deeply into an assessment of whether we are operating at the level of "best practice" in everything we do. The concept of "best practice" should be derived from both internal and external policing experts and, most importantly, from the members of the communities that we serve. When gaps are identified we must immediately remediate and reform. This continuous gap analysis falls directly on the Risk Management Bureau, whose mission was envisioned to be the tip of the spear in reform.

We should recognize all the more clearly during these times of heightened scrutiny that the role and responsibilities of

RMB in the Department must be elevated, not diminished. The Bureau should be the primary liaison with all oversight entities. Moreover, the risk management process of identifying, analyzing, and collaboratively developing remediation of risks to the Department, and then monitoring those risks to ensure compliance with remediation, must lie at the heart of our reform efforts.

Simply put, RMB must ask the tough questions and deliver the, sometimes harsh, reality. Recent discussions, however, relative to diminishing RMB's role in the process, are, I respectfully suggest, severely misplaced and run counter to the reform that the Department is trying to achieve. The Risk Management Bureau's mission is very different than that of the Legal Bureau. DCLM's role has always been to protect the organization from liability and has not been institutionally or bureaucratically attuned to appreciate that remediation of the factors underlying potential liability, and cooperation with oversight entities, even if embarrassing or potentially costly in the short term, have significant long-term beneficial effects. The overall improvement of our Department far outweighs any short-term harm from an embarrassment, a liability payout on an individual case, or a potential detrimental effect on a specific officer's ability to testify by virtue of the application of rules dealing with disclosure of police witnesses' backgrounds.

The recent dispute regarding whether RMB should be specifically requesting prosecutors and potentially the CCRB and IAB to bring to the attention of the Early Intervention Program those officers who they believe should be immediately reviewed for potential non-disciplinary intervention, including mentoring, additional training, and enhanced supervision, highlights the problem. Rather than learn about an officer whose career might be saved and, moreover, whose risk to the Department and potentially the public might be diminished or removed, the Department is considering not requesting such referrals thereby dissuading them because such referral could ultimately be used as Giglio

> material when an officer is called to testify. Such a course, in my opinion, runs extremely contrary to the interests of the City and of the Department.
>
> Over my three years at NYPD, I have often felt like the Lorax in Dr. Seuss's book. I have always tried, as best I could, to respectfully promote what I saw as needed change in the Department. In that role, I internalized the Lorax mission: "Unless someone like you cares a whole awful lot, nothing is going to get better. It's not." But I have come to realize that caring alone is not enough. We must all fully understand and internalize where we have gone wrong and what we need to do to have things get better and put us squarely on the path to policing in a fair, just, transparent, and accountable way.
>
> I have never met a more caring and dedicated Executive Staff than you, Commissioner Tucker, and my colleagues. It has been my privilege and honor to work with you and them and to be a small part of the history of the NYPD. Of course, going forward I will always be more than happy to help you and the Department in any way I possibly can.
>
> With many thanks,
>
> Jeff Schlanger
> Deputy Commissioner, Risk Management Bureau

I thought the letter was respectful, direct, and final.

I left quietly in the spring of 2021. I knew then, as I know now, that change within an institution like the NYPD is never easy. It is incremental, often met with resistance, and frequently misunderstood. But that does not make it any less vital. Reform is not a moment—it is a process. And in my time at the NYPD, I was honored to be part of that process.

The compounded stress of civil unrest, pandemic losses, long tours, and institutional skepticism made this one of the most difficult periods in the Department's history. Officers felt both demonized and abandoned, and even the most committed reformers within the agency struggled with the burden of pushing for accountability while holding the line on public safety. But it was also a period of profound clarity—about the limits of existing structures, the price of inertia, and the pressing need for reform not only in words, but in action.

I left with no regrets, only the hope that what we began would continue to grow in the hands of those willing to carry it forward.

Within weeks of my departure, the Civil Rights Integrity Unit that I had set up to specifically and directly address the level of constitutional policing within the Department was disbanded. Matt Pontillo was given a third star and took over the mantle at RMB. And while I knew the Bureau was in excellent hands, I also knew that without the right person at the top, the best intentions of the Risk Management Bureau would not address the issues that continued to plague the Department. At the time, though, I did not yet know how far the Department would fall.

Chapter 40
Integrity Assurance

When I left the NYPD in March 2021, it didn't feel like stepping away from the work. It felt like stepping back into it—on my own terms.

My wife and I had been talking for years about building a life in Florida. Warmer weather, more time together, and less of the institutional grind overall. We made it real almost immediately. We drove south, settled into our condo, established Florida as our legal residence, and began treating New York as a place we went to visit—not where we lived. After four decades of being tethered to large public institutions, it was the first time in my career that I could decide which problems to take on, and on what terms.

Almost as soon as the boxes were unpacked, I started building what came next.

I formed IntegrAssure.

The premise behind IntegrAssure was simple to describe and hard to execute: that any policing agency—large or small, crisis-ridden or well-regarded—can build a culture of integrity if it commits to structured, transparent, continuous improvement. Not "check-the-box" compliance. Not glossy reform messaging. Actual, verifiable improvement.

The name was intentional. I wanted it to sound like what it is: integrity assurance. Assurance not in the PR sense, but in the audit sense—an obligation to examine risk honestly, fix what's fixable, change what isn't working, and then prove you did it.

In the beginning, the firm was just me, my laptop, and a set of frameworks I had been developing for years. I drafted proposals, built templates, and formalized what I had spent a career doing informally: assessing risk, measuring behavior, forcing systems to confront the gap between their policy and their practice, and then standing next to them as they tried to close it.

Very quickly, I wasn't alone. Erin Pilnyak—who had worked with me at the NYPD—joined me in the early phase and helped with project management and client delivery. Over time, our approaches diverged, and we agreed to part ways in early 2024. Others have been with me for decades as well. Denise Lewis and Hazel deBurgh, for example, have been in the fight with me in one form or another since the LAPD. A new addition to the team, Dayna Schock, a Coast Guard veteran with a broad range of experience and talent, joined the company, as both a subject matter expert and business manager. The team is small, but it's extraordinary. It has to be. You don't walk into a police department and ask it to change if you're not bringing people who know exactly what they're doing.

In its first years, IntegrAssure found its footing fast. We advised on accountability structures in New York, Colorado, Connecticut, and elsewhere. We conducted use-of-force reviews for the federal government. And we took on three core long-term roles that, taken together, capture what I believe modern police oversight should be: Independent Monitor in Aurora, Colorado; and, Independent Police Auditor in both San Leandro and Petaluma, California.

Aurora: State-Mandated Reform

When I began work in Aurora, what struck me most was not its size or complexity, but the whiplash of its public narrative.

Few police departments in modern memory have experienced such a dramatic reversal of sentiment. In 2012, after the mass shooting inside an Aurora movie theater, its officers were hailed as heroes—steady, decisive, and courageous under unimaginable pressure. Less than seven years later, after the in-custody-death of an autistic 23-year-old, those same uniforms had become symbols of mistrust and misconduct. What made Aurora so striking was that transformation: from unquestioned heroism to vilification, from public gratitude to public outrage, all within a single decade.

The origin was a tragedy.

On August 24, 2019, Aurora police officers stopped Elijah McClain, a 23-year-old Black man walking home from a convenience store. A 911 caller had labeled him "suspicious" because he was wearing a ski mask on a warm night. McClain was unarmed. He had committed no crime. He was, by all accounts, gentle, idiosyncratic, and physically fragile; he wore the mask because he was anemic and often cold.

Within minutes, the encounter spiraled. Officers forced him to the ground, applied a carotid hold, and pinned him prone. When Aurora Fire Rescue arrived, paramedics injected him with 500 milligrams of ketamine. Shortly afterward, McClain went into cardiac arrest. He died days later.

The initial local review cleared the officers and the paramedics. The anger over that decision, which began in Aurora, exploded statewide after the murder of George Floyd in 2020. Under intense public pressure, Governor Jared Polis directed the Colorado Attorney General, Phil Weiser, to launch a civil rights investigation into the Aurora Police Department.

In September 2021, the Attorney General's office issued its findings. The report concluded that Aurora PD had engaged in a pattern and practice of racially biased policing, unconstitutional force, and discriminatory enforcement. It also identified dangerous practices within Aurora Fire Rescue—most notably, the administration of sedatives like ketamine in the field.

Rather than litigate, the City of Aurora entered into a court-enforceable Consent Decree. The decree did something unusual: it covered both the Police Department and the Fire Department. It required not only sweeping changes to policies, training, use of force and stops, but also to medical practice and field sedation. In 2022, the IntegrAssure team, with me as the designated Independent Monitor, was chosen by the City and the Attorney General's Office to oversee that process.

Aurora has tested every lesson I've ever learned about reform.

First, leadership instability. Since we began oversight, the department has cycled through a series of chiefs. That level of turnover makes reform exponentially harder. You don't just lose continuity. You lose credibility—inside the department and in the community.

Some of those changes were purely transitional; some reflected deeper philosophical differences. Dan Oates, a former Aurora chief (and former NYPD executive), returned as interim chief to stabilize the department. He brought institutional familiarity, which helped in some ways, but, as an interim solution, was not oriented toward long-term structural reform.

He was followed by Art Acevedo, formerly chief in Austin and Houston. Art and I had clashed years earlier over my findings in the two officer-involved shootings in Austin related earlier in this book. But we buried that in the first week in Aurora. He, too, came in as an interim chief and, to his credit, pushed urgently on compliance. With him came a deputy, Heather Morris, who, after Art left, carried reforms forward during yet another interim period.

The City then launched a national search. City Manager Jason Batchelor, with the help of senior city attorney Pete Schulte (who went on to become City Attorney), selected a permanent chief: Todd Chamberlain, a former LAPD commander. His appointment drew criticism because the process did not include public input. The community's frustration was understandable, but so too was the City Manager's position. Prior attempts to fill the role had become politicized, with candidates evaluated less on their overall qualifications and more on isolated aspects of their background or beliefs. Jason was determined to avoid that dynamic. He wanted a chief who could meet as many of the City's and the Department's needs as possible, and he concluded that such a search could not succeed under the glare and division that a public process would inevitably generate.

But once in the chair, Chamberlain did the single most important thing a chief can do under a consent decree: he made it clear, internally, that compliance wasn't optional. He is direct. He is steady. He understands morale. He has moved the department forward in measurable ways.

The second test has been expectation management. The community—especially those closest to the Elijah McClain case—wanted to see seismic change immediately. I understood that. I also knew, from LAPD and NYPD, that institutional reform is not a sprint. Once installed as Monitor, I created a Community Advisory Council to act as a conduit between myself as Monitor and the community and to help explain that the Consent Decree has a five-year term for a reason. You are rewiring muscle memory. You don't do that in five news cycles' worth.

The third test is broader than Aurora: can a department not only reach compliance, but stay there without constant federal or state pressure? That is the real question. And it is why leadership matters more than language. Policies, after all, look great in binders. Culture is what happens at 2:30 a.m. on a dark street.

As of now, Aurora is on track to hit substantial compliance within the anticipated five-year window. But the more important outcome is this: the department is positioning itself to become, not the cautionary tale in Colorado, but the model.

I've come to believe, more strongly than at any point in my career, that the overwhelming majority of officers want to do their job honorably. When they are given clear expectations, backed by fair supervision, and led by people who mean what they say, they will meet that standard.

Petaluma: Foresight and Oversight

Petaluma, in many ways, is the counterpoint to Aurora.

In 2022, the City of Petaluma, in Sonoma County, brought me in as its Independent Police Auditor. What made Petaluma notable was what didn't happen. There was no viral use-of-force video. No in-custody death. No federal investigation.

Instead, city leadership—the City Manager, City Council, and the Chief of Police—decided that independent oversight was simply the right thing to build.

That may sound unremarkable. It isn't. Most cities adopt oversight because they're forced to. Petaluma did it because they believed proactive auditing, transparency, and outside review of force, pursuits, internal investigations, and body-worn camera footage would make them better.

Our work there focuses on exactly that: policy review and use-of-force, pursuit, and complaint investigation assessments. We don't wait for a scandal. We look for risk. We surface it. We resolve it while it's still small.

If Aurora is about rebuilding trust after a breach, Petaluma is about protecting trust before it breaks.

San Leandro: Before the Feds

San Leandro, a city of 80,000 bordering Oakland, came to independent oversight the way most cities do: through tragedy.

On April 18, 2020, Steven Taylor, a 33-year-old Black man experiencing a mental health crisis, was shot and killed by a San Leandro officer inside a Walmart. Taylor was holding a baseball bat. The body-worn camera footage shows an encounter that escalated rapidly and ended in gunfire that many in the community believed was unnecessary and avoidable.

The shooting triggered intense public anger and raised deep questions about proportionality, tactics, de-escalation, and crisis response.

In the aftermath, San Leandro created a new oversight model and appointed me—through IntegrAssure—as Independent Police

Auditor. My role there includes reviewing critical incidents, use-of-force investigations, pursuits, complaints and policy; engaging with the city's community review structure; and identifying structural gaps—the places where training, supervision, or practice are not aligned with constitutional policing.

What I've seen in San Leandro is familiar: departments in the aftermath of a high-profile incident often say they are committed to change. The question is whether they will invite scrutiny when the cameras are gone. San Leandro has and continues to.

Coming Full Circle

Midway into the Aurora monitorship, in October 2024, came the moment that reframed everything: the birth of our first grandchild, Shai. I remember standing in the hospital room, the Colorado mountains still fresh in my mind from the week before and holding him for the first time. His entire hand wrapped around my little finger, and I felt an overwhelming sense of continuity—of the responsibilities passed from one generation to the next.

As I looked down at him, I thought about the cases I had handled, the agencies I had helped reform, and the officers and families whose lives had intersected with mine along the way. In that small, perfect moment, all of it converged into a simple truth: the work we do, the choices we make, matter most when measured through the eyes of those who will inherit the world we leave behind. Shai was only hours old, yet he sharpened my understanding of why doing right—quietly, consistently, without concession—matters more than ever.

In some ways, IntegrAssure brought me back to where I started with Corplex decades ago: standing slightly outside institutions, close enough to understand it, yet far enough to tell it the truth.

The tools are sharper now — body-worn cameras, real-time analytics, early intervention systems, and risk dashboards that can track an officer's trajectory in a way no chief could have imagined in 1990. But the questions haven't changed.

Are you policing constitutionally?

Are you treating people with dignity?

Are you learning from the last bad outcome so you don't repeat it?

And are you willing to let someone independent verify that?

That last part—willingness to be seen—remains, in 2025, the dividing line. Departments that open themselves to honest examination tend to get better. Departments that retreat behind rhetoric tend not to.

I think about this a lot. I run a small firm built on the idea that accountability and improvement can be delivered through collaboration instead of litigation. Some days, I wonder whether that's enough—whether small, persistent work can really bend institutions into best practices

Then I watch a department like Petaluma ask for oversight before it's forced. I watch a place like Aurora, after a death that shocked the conscience of the country, stabilize around expectations of professionalism instead of improvisation. I watch a city like San Leandro commit, in public, to examining its most painful moment.

And I come to the same conclusion I've come to, in one form or another, throughout my entire career. If done correctly, the small, persistent work of risk management, of integrity assurance, can, in fact, reduce liabilities and make an institution and those who work within it, immeasurably better.

I don't pretend to have all the answers. But I know the work. The work is to identify risk early, not after a disaster. The work is to insist on dignity as a condition of authority. The work is to measure, document, and improve—openly. And the work is to do that collaboratively, with humility, asking in every case the only question that actually matters:

What could we have done better to get a better outcome?

That's still the job.

Chapter 41
The Weight of Certainty

It was the summer of 2025.

The air in New York carried that heavy mix of heat and impatience that always seems to settle over the city by July. I was in the family's summer home in Quogue, splitting my professional time between Aurora, Petaluma, and San Leandro—moving from one reform effort to another—when a text from my longtime friend Joel Rudin appeared on my phone.

"Hi Jeff. I just recommended you to Earl Ward as a potential expert witness on police and prosecutorial practice."

That was all it said. No background, no preamble—just Joel, concise and direct, as he had always been.

We'd met nearly fifty years earlier in the Criminal Law Clinic at NYU, two young idealists trying to make the law mean something more than precedent and punishment. Our lives had diverged but had never drifted apart.

Joel stayed on the defense side, carving out a national reputation for exonerating the wrongly convicted. I took the other path—into the Manhattan District Attorney's Office—where ambition burned brightly, but the moral compass was anchored by Robert Morgenthau's steady insistence: do what's right.

That simple text from Joel was enough to tell me the matter would touch the edges of that moral terrain.

A few days later, Earl Ward called. Earl had spent his early career at Legal Aid, practicing at 100 Centre Street, just a few years behind me. He laughed as soon as we connected.

"I remember you back then," he said. "You were the big, feared prosecutor—the guy we used to warn our clients about."

We both laughed. Those days were long past. He was still fighting for those who couldn't fight for themselves, and I had spent decades trying to repair the systems that had failed them. In our own ways, we had both become custodians of justice.

Earl explained that he was representing Anthony Broadwater, the man wrongfully convicted of raping Alice Sebold, the author of *Lucky* and other literary works. The case had become infamous: a young white college student assaulted in 1981, a Black man determined to be wrongly convicted through revelations in the victim's book recounting the incident, and four decades later, a judicial acknowledgment that everything about that prosecution had been flawed. Earl asked if I would serve as an expert witness in the civil rights suit against Onondaga County, focusing on police and prosecutorial conduct.

Even before reviewing the file, I felt the weight of it.

What struck me most, once I began reading, was not complexity but fragility. In my view, the case rested on no reliable evidence—no credible identification, no physical proof, no meaningful corroboration. What remained was a mistaken identification, prosecutorial decisions that ignored the limits of that evidence, and a detective's silence at critical moments when those weaknesses were apparent.

The facts, as they emerged through Ms. Sebold's own recollection in her memoir *Lucky* and in subsequent court records and depositions, painted a devastating picture. My professional opinion—like every conclusion in my expert report—rested on those accounts.

In May 1981, Sebold, then eighteen and a student at Syracuse University, was raped by a stranger in Thornden Park. She described her assailant as a young Black man, about five-foot-six, muscular, with a short afro. Five months later, she saw a man on the street whom she believed to be her attacker. That man was Anthony

Broadwater.

He was arrested shortly thereafter. But when a lineup was held, Sebold failed to identify him. Instead, she pointed to another participant in the lineup—a filler—whom the prosecutor herself had noted was dissimilar to Broadwater in appearance.

According to Sebold's account, recorded in *Lucky*, the prosecutor and the detective indicated afterward that she had "picked the wrong one." The prosecutor, angry, explained that the two men were "dead ringers," that they were "friends" who "always used each other in lineups," and that "[they] got the hair from the bastard"—a reference to a pubic hair sample taken immediately after the lineup, intimating that it somehow linked Broadwater to the crime.

Every one of those statements was, as later records and testimony made clear, inaccurate or misleading. The two men were strangers; the hair analysis had not yet been performed; and even once it was, it could show only that the hair was 'consistent with' Broadwater's—not that it came from him.

Still, the case was presented to a grand jury that same day. Broadwater was indicted and, the following spring, convicted at a bench trial. He served sixteen and a half years in prison.

As I read through the transcripts, I was disheartened—not simply as an expert, but as someone who had spent a career believing that good faith and professionalism could guard against catastrophe.

What happened in Syracuse wasn't a mystery; it was, in my view, a failure of professional restraint. The prosecutor and detective had every opportunity to recognize that the identification had failed. The case should have ended there. Instead, the evidence was framed in a way that gave way to continued prosecution rather than fully accounting its weaknesses.

That impulse—to bend ambiguity into certainty—is one every

prosecutor knows. And it's one that can only be resisted if humility outweighs ambition.

When I met with Joel a few weeks later—after I had already begun drafting my report—we didn't dwell on the case's facts. Instead, we talked about the larger legal principles it raised: the erosion of probable cause after a failed identification, the ethical duty to disclose exculpatory information, and the fine line between investigation and advocacy.

It felt almost like being back in the clinic again—two students parsing the moral code of prosecution, except now we carried decades of experience and scar tissue between us. Over the years we had often discussed how the pursuit of justice can become self-justifying, how the "win" can quietly replace the truth, and how even well-intentioned prosecutors can lose sight of the line between advocacy and distortion.

We both knew how little it had taken to destroy Broadwater's life—a unaddressed mistaken identification, a handful of words uttered in frustration, and forty years of silence before justice found him.

As I wrote my report, I kept returning to one truth: serious misconduct can arise even when people believe they are acting with the best of intentions. The assistant district attorney in that case wasn't a caricature of corruption; she appears, from the record, to have been a young prosecutor trying to hold together a fragile case. The detective wasn't a villain; rather, he was complacent at moments when vigilance was required. Together they created the perfect storm of error—a failure that met every legal definition of a due-process violation but also revealed the psychological fragility of the system itself.

Even under the rule of law, good people can and do make ruinous mistakes.

My expert opinion was simple: once Ms. Sebold failed to identify Broadwater in the lineup, any arguable probable cause to prosecute him, in my view, was no longer present. The decision to continue the prosecution—in which an identification of the second choice in the lineup was tainted with the narrative of 'dead ringers' and on hair comparison testimony that could not reliably identify Broadwater as the source—constituted, in my opinion, unethical and unconstitutional conduct. The detective's silence in the face of those weaknesses compounded the harm. The failure to make the defense aware of the taint violated not just ethical standards but well-established law on the duty of a prosecutor to make the defense aware of exculpatory evidence. Taken together, the actions fell, in my judgment, well short of the professional standards governing prosecutors and police officers in 1981.

But what stayed with me wasn't the legal finding; it was the human cost.

As I reflected on it, I found myself comparing the Broadwater case to one that had defined an earlier part of my career: the prosecution of Mickey Featherstone, detailed earlier in the Westies chapter.

That case, too, had begun with certainty. We knew Featherstone had murdered Michael Holly. The evidence was strong, the narrative airtight. I was sure of it—until we discovered it wasn't true.

But when Featherstone claimed he had been framed, we didn't dismiss him. We reopened the investigation, scrutinized our own work, and found that he was right. He had been set up. We admitted our mistake, and his conviction was vacated.

The way in which those two cases were handled is instructive. In one, we questioned ourselves and immediately corrected the wrong. In the other, the State doubled down and perpetuated it for forty years. Justice should not have to wait that long.

The difference wasn't moral superiority; it was culture. Under Morgenthau, doubt wasn't a weakness—it was a duty. In some offices driven by political ambition or institutional insecurity, success is too often measured by conviction tallies. DANY, at its best, measured it by conscience.

It's not that we were immune to error. It's that we were allowed to admit it.

When I filed my expert report that September, it concluded that both the assistant district attorney and the detective had violated the professional standards of their time, but what I could not include in the report was the deeper truth that animated it: that law, like democracy, survives only when people within it are willing to question their own certainty.

Featherstone had taught me that lesson decades earlier. Broadwater reminded me again.

Chapter 42

The Hard Part of Doing Right

As I reflect on the Sebold case, one realization lingered: even a culture built on integrity can fray and erode under misguided leadership.

Over the past decade, I've watched the rule of law strain under the weight of politics and expedience. What happened in Syracuse in 1981 was one of its failures—a miscarriage born of human frailty, and a reminder that the law alone is never enough; it takes people willing to do what is right to keep it whole.

What we have witnessed in recent years is something far more dangerous in its potentially ubiquitous impact: a fraying of the rule of law itself, as certainty is weaponized not to convict the guilty, but to shield the powerful and punish the inconvenient. Evidence is mocked, truth distorted, and the impartial machinery of justice is pulled into the orbit of partisanship. The damage begins at the top, but it does not stay there. It seeps downward—into city halls, police departments, and courtrooms—reshaping how people understand fairness itself.

I saw it firsthand at the NYPD: the tension between accountability and expedience, between the desire to do right and the confusion of those who no longer knew what "right" meant. After my departure, under the Adams administration, things got exponentially worse. What had once been isolated lapses began to look like institutional practice.

The Broadwater case reminded me that even in a functioning system, injustice can take root. The last ten years have shown me that when the system itself loses its moral foundation, injustice can become policy.

That foundation—the moral credo on which the rule of law depends—cannot be legal doctrine alone. It must rest on shared human values.

When I wrote an op-ed in 2021 for the New York Daily News, I called for policing to adopt a simple moral compass—one that could serve as a Hippocratic Oath for those who wield the power of the state. I argued that humanity, integrity, and empathy must be policing's north stars, and that every officer should swear fidelity to those ideals as surely as to the Constitution.

Later, in developing curricula for IntegrAssure's clients, we gave that compass form and called them the CHIEF Directives: Courage, Humanity, Integrity, and Empathy—For All.

Courage, to act ethically even when it is inconvenient or dangerous.

Humanity, to treat every person with dignity, both in word and in deed.

Integrity, to remain truthful and honest, even when truth comes at a cost.

Empathy, to see others as we would want ourselves and our families to be seen.

For All—to apply these principles universally, without prejudice or bias.

These are not just the foundation of public safety; they are the architecture of the rule of law itself. Remove them, and all other reforms—whether in policing, prosecution, or politics—collapse under the weight of cynicism and self-interest.

Even when the rule of law functions, justice often moves slowly. When the rule of law itself deteriorates, justice does not move at all.

Looking back across more than four and a half decades—from

the adrenaline of prosecution to the patience of oversight—I've come to understand that doing the right thing is not a single act, but a discipline. It demands patience when anger would be easier, humility when certainty feels safer, and courage when silence would cost less.

Reform within large institutions is always possible—but only if there is the will to face uncomfortable truths. At the NYPD, I saw how bureaucracy and self-protection can dull that will, even among good people. The challenge was never about rules or policies; it was about the courage to apply them with integrity.

That has been the thread through my life—from Valley Stream to the courtroom, from the DA's Office to One Police Plaza. We cannot always control outcomes, but we can control our conduct—how we act, what we stand for, and whether we leave the world a little fairer than we found it.

Justice, as it turns out, is tested in the everyday decisions where authority and pressure collide with what is fair and right. Those are the moments when empathy has to guide power, and when integrity—not convenience—determines whether the system works.

We can repair the cracks of an imperfect system, even if the work takes time. But when the foundation itself crumbles under deliberate assault, there may very well be nothing left to rebuild.

In the end, the only safeguard is conscience—and an enduring promise by each of us to do what's right, and to hold one another accountable when we don't.

Epilogue

As this book goes to press, the nation stands at a fragile edge between law and power. The rule of law—so long our bulwark against chaos—is being tested in ways not seen since the Civil War, not by misunderstanding or error, but by deliberate defiance. Prosecutors and judges are threatened for doing their jobs. Truth is bartered for advantage. Facts themselves have become contested terrain. The system endures, but whether it holds will depend on the choices we make next.

We are at a critical point in our history—a moment that will likely determine whether the country recommits to the rule of law or continues to treat it as a partisan convenience. The choices are not for politicians alone, but for all of us: whether we still believe that facts matter, that decency counts, and that truth is not something to be negotiated.

That corrosion is not confined to any one city or institution. It is visible, too, in the growing entanglement of federal immigration enforcement with local policing—where fear replaces trust, accountability gives way to opacity, and the line between law enforcement and political coercion blurs. In Minneapolis, that breakdown ended not in reform or restraint, but in the killings of Renee Good and Alex Pretti, a reminder that when institutions abandon clarity of purpose and moral restraint, the consequences are borne not by abstractions, but by people.

That tension has also been visible in New York City—the place that first taught me what the law demands. There, under the Adams administration, the corrosion of conscience was evident at every level of government. For the NYPD, the Adams years will be remembered as among the darkest since the days of Serpico and the "Dirty Thirty." Scandals reached senior levels of city government, with a deputy mayor, a commissioner, and a chief of department stepping down amid intense public scrutiny and controversy. It was a period when the city's moral compass spun wildly, and those who had once pledged to serve the public were seen by many as, instead, serving themselves.

Yet even in that turbulence, the outline of renewal began to appear. Under the threat of removal by the Governor, Mayor Adams appointed Jessica Tisch—a leader I know well and deeply respect from our shared years at the NYPD. She understood, as Morgenthau once did, that doing right is not a slogan but a practice—a discipline measured not by popularity or politics, but by integrity. Her leadership began the slow work of rebuilding the department's foundation, grounded in ethics and accountability.

Whether that culture of conscience endures will depend on what follows. Mayor Zohran Mamdani, who kept Commissioner Tisch in place, faces a question larger than politics: not just how to lead a city, but how to protect its soul. The work of justice will always be imperfect, but it must never be abandoned—and that begins with putting the right people in the right places—those willing to do right when it matters most.

Tribulations like those in Minneapolis and New York, have a way of teaching what no law book ever could. They remind us that the law alone can't guarantee justice—that justice depends, always, on the conscience of those who live and work within it. In every precinct and courtroom, and in the quiet moments when no one is watching, doing right is what gives the law meaning and keeps faith with those it serves.

The story of the NYPD, New York City, Minneapolis, and the nation is, of course, still being written. Whether the next chapters record decline or renewal will depend on whether we can summon the courage, humanity, integrity, and empathy for all—to do right. Those are, after all, the living threads that bind principle to power and hold justice together when everything else begins to fray.

The work of strengthening institutions was never abstract to me. It played out in the very real rhythms of my own life, often demanding time, travel, and a level of presence that came at the expense of moments at home.

Over the course of my career, the work often required long stretches away from home. During the LAPD Consent Decree, the HSBC monitorship, and many other assignments around the world, I spent more time in airports and hotel rooms than I ever expected when I first entered public service. While I was away, life in New York moved on without me. I missed snowstorms that shut down the city, floods that filled basements (including ours), and hurricanes that sent neighbors checking on one another. And, most significantly, I was not home on 9/11. Like millions of others, I watched the images on television, but I did so from a distance, separated from my family and my city at the moment it needed unity most.

T held things together during those years, managing the day-to-day realities for our family without complaint. The kids grew, their routines continued, and whatever disruptions came—weather, school closures, or emergencies—she handled them. She didn't just manage the logistics; she managed the emotional landscape I was often too absent to tend. When I was taking conference calls outside an emergency room or stuck in a hotel in Los Angeles while the world burned on 9/11, she was the one creating safety for our children. I see now that my ability to do right in the world was entirely dependent on her doing right by our family, every single day.

Looking back across a lifetime—from Valley Stream to Manhattan's courts and through the many roles that followed—I see that the work, in all its forms, came down to a single obligation: to try to do right when it mattered. Not perfectly, not without missteps, but with a commitment to fairness, to truth, and to the belief that institutions function best when those inside them strive for continuous improvement and hold themselves accountable. That has been the constant through-line of my career. But ultimately, doing right isn't about the cases you win or the policies you rewrite.

It's about the world you leave behind. It is my hope that when we step away, the institutions we built are strong enough to hold, and the people coming next—my children, my grandchildren, and yours—inherit a system that is just a little more fair and just than the one we found.

Index

Names and Organizations

Roman numerals refer to front matter pages.

A

B

C

D

E

F

G

H

I

J

K

L

M

N

O

P

Q

R

S

T

U

V

W

Y

Z

www.ingramcontent.com/pod-product-compliance
Ingram Content Group UK Ltd.
Pitfield, Milton Keynes, MK11 3LW, UK
UKHW062155030826
14089UKWH00026B/35

9 798995 407911